Testimony *of a* Miracle Man

JOSEPH CALLIHAN

ISBN 978-1-64191-140-5 (paperback)
ISBN 978-1-64191-141-2 (digital)

Copyright © 2018 by Joseph Callihan

All rights reserved. No part of this publication may be reproduced, distributed, or transmitted in any form or by any means, including photocopying, recording, or other electronic or mechanical methods without the prior written permission of the publisher. For permission requests, solicit the publisher via the address below.

Christian Faith Publishing, Inc.
832 Park Avenue
Meadville, PA 16335
www.christianfaithpublishing.com

Printed in the United States of America

CONTENTS

Brief Note Regarding Grammar 7
Foreword.. 9
Introduction... 13
Chapter 1   Why Me? 15
Chapter 2   It All Began with
            Severe Headaches 19
Chapter 3   The Power and Fun of Being a
            Witness for God........................... 24
Chapter 4   Getting a Second Opinion 31
Oncologist Report... 35
Chapter 5   New Doctors Arrive
            on the Scene................................. 36
Chapter 6   A "Fun" Return Visit and satan Gets
            Involved 50
Chapter 7   The Good, Bad, and Ugly Lies 54
Medical Records.. 57
Chapter 8   Alcohol and Me:
            The True Story 64

Chapter 9	One More Alcohol and Me: True Story	76
Chapter 10	Update: My Fourth Death Proclamation Is Issued	81
Chapter 11	Man Who Hears from God	86
Chapter 12	Hurt Feelings, Misconceived Pride, and Unusual Man of God	97
Chapter 13	Chemo: The "Miracle" Drug	101
Chapter 14	Faith: The Two-Sided Coin	108
One Last Request		115
Poem 1	The Only Thing Left to Do	119
Poem 2	Growing Faith	120
Poem 3	I CRY OUT	122
My Personal Confession		125
Poem 4	HELP IS ON THE WAY	132
Poem 5	Psalm of a Man Told by Doctors He is Dying	134

HOLY BIBLE

℞

Romans 8:28, 35–39
1 John 4:18
Psalm 91:14–16
1 Peter 5:9–10
Psalm 30: 1–5

In You do I live, breathe, move, and have my being
PERFECT LOVE CASTS OUT FEAR

Joe Callihan

BRIEF NOTE REGARDING GRAMMAR

I am a bit different among authors, especially as most of my books are of Christian nature and subject. As a matter of respect for the Lord, God, I tend to break certain rules of grammar intentionally. I absolutely refuse to use a capital letter whenever naming satan, lucifer, his demons, or his domain (hell). I don't care if it is at the beginning of a sentence, or whose rules it may be breaking, be it Chicago's or those of anyone else's rules of proper grammar.

Out of my disdain for my spiritual enemy, satan, and the greatest of due respect for my God, I will never permit any honor being given in my books to satan, lucifer, or the devil and his evil minions. I operate on what I deem to be spiritually correct use of grammar. As both a boy and later a man, whenever faced with having to deal with one trying to bully me, I always have believed it to be foolish to show any form of respect to the bully. Rather

I belittled and made all kinds of deliberate disrespectful fun of everything they said. I wanted them to clearly understand we were enemies, and if they unwisely choose to go to war with me, there would be hell to pay. I have always had this same attitude toward satan, times a million.

I refuse to have my name put on a book which shows any kind of honor or respect to satan. Likewise, I refuse to have my name on any book, which fails to show honor, praise, and glory to my Lord and the King of Kings.

I am aware the "perfectionist" may not like my attitude. That's OK, because I understand their lack of spiritual maturity, which would make them take such a stand. It is my hope and prayer, after having read my testimony from cover to cover, their spiritual understanding of who God is, how mighty His mercy is, how great His perfect love is for us, and what a little worm satan and his demons are. It will give them insight into the worthiness of offering praise to God and spit on the devil, our mutual enemy.

FOREWORD

In the same way, no one has knowledge of the things of God but the Spirit of God.

—1 Corinthians 2

The book you are about to read is a remarkable testimony of what *true faith* and the fruit of that faith really look like. However, in my humble opinion, the average reader without significant medical knowledge will fail to see how miraculous this story really is. This is the reason why yours truly was chosen by God, not the author, to write this *foreword*. When you are done with this book, many will say, "Wow, I know someone like that."

Joseph prayed to the Holy Spirit and asked Him, "Whom have You chosen to write the *foreword* for this book?" I know that, because I know Joe. So when he asked me to do so, not only was it an honor, as his physician for several years now, but it was also a duty as a Christian. I couldn't say no, and I couldn't say, "Let me pray on this and get back to you." There was no escaping this.

Medicine is my calling. This is why God put me on His Earth, to serve His children in my capacity as an internal medicine physician. I have been in practice for seventeen years in the Tampa Bay area serving mostly a geriatric population. For the last ten years, I have also been teaching residents and students. I have acquired much knowledge and expertise, and despite everything I have been exposed to, I continue to be in *awe* of God's power and majesty. As A. W. Tozer said in his book, *The Knowledge of the Holy*, "God is incomprehensible!"

Twelve months after a hospitalization at a Veterans Administration hospital for several life-threatening complications, Joseph was diagnosed with multiple myeloma. His hospitalization was due to complications from one of the highest levels of calcium in the blood that I have seen. He should not have left the hospital alive—yes, *alive*—let alone walk around the streets of St. Petersburg with calcium levels around 13–14 mg/dL for a whole year before the diagnosis.

When I first saw Joe, I didn't know what to think. I was worried that the elevated calcium was playing tricks on his mind. High calcium levels can cause confusion and also hallucinations and psychosis. I have seen God perform so many miracles in seventeen years that I could write a book about it. So while I already knew without any treatment he should have been either dead or have some cognitive impairment, I wanted to make sure he was not demented.

So in April of 2014, after all the testing was done including a bone marrow biopsy (which we begged him to get done), I had a discussion with the oncologist. We confirmed the multiple myeloma had spread to his bones, liver, and spleen. It was also affecting his kidneys that were functioning at about 20 percent or so. Just as a side note, when the function is less than 15 percent, you need dialysis. Some of the cancer markers that determine if the tumor is aggressive or not all came back stating it was "very aggressive." I don't even know why I was surprised at this.

After all, when God decides to intervene, He does it under a circumstance that leaves no doubt whatsoever He was involved.

So when Joe came to the office, I laid all the evidence before him and just flat out told him, "Medicine cannot explain why you are alive. As Sir William Osler said once, 'Medicine is a science of uncertainty and an art of probability.'"

Knowing this, I have made a decision in my life to let faith support me where reason fails. I have seen reason fail many times, and I happily give God the credit. This is one of the areas where I get frustrated with many of my colleagues. We often talk about patients that lived four years instead of two years. Some patients walk when we thought they never would. Stroke patients speak more eloquently than the best of speakers. Yet despite all this, only a handful agree with me when I give the credit to God. Most just get nervous and change the topic.

Fast forward to July 2017 and my patient and friend is not just alive. He is doing great. The tumor has fallen asleep like the lions slumbered next to Daniel in the den. He should have been on dialysis two to three years ago, but his kidneys are still functioning exactly the same. His calcium goes up to about 13.5 and sometimes is totally normal. There have been many times when I see Joe, and after he leaves the visit, I wonder if this will be the last time I get to see what we call in the office, "our miracle man." But when I do see him, I smile and think about our wonderful God.

May God bless the reader of this book as He has blessed Joe.

Miguel Fana Jr., MD, CPC, CPCO

INTRODUCTION

Here, I must apologize for being unprepared. You'd think I would know better. However, sadly, I failed to consider the time restraints placed in getting a book to market in a timely manner. I discovered me having failed to ask my pastor friends early enough, to write the introduction. The need to get the manuscript to the publisher, with any hope of possibly marketing during the upcoming Christmas season, was urgent.

As a result, I, the author, am now going to attempt to write an introduction which I hope will offer the reader intrigue needed to be eager to read these stories of miracles I have encountered and, prayerfully, an understanding of the depth of spiritual growth, which may be obtained by readers, to be found in the truths revealed within the pages of this book.

As the author, I humbly am simply being used as God's reporter of "good news." The application of faith, a gift we all are given by God, can and does indeed move mountains. My testimony is all for the honor and glory of Father God, Jesus, and the Holy Spirit. In these stories, you can see the works of the Father in bringing needed answers to sincere prayer. You also will clearly see how the power of the precious blood of my Savior, restoring my relationship with my Heavenly Father, makes it possible for me to boldly approach Him in His throne room and make my petitions known. Lastly, you will see how I desperately needed the guidance of the Comforter as He ministered peace, joy, and a sound mind to me.

    I hope I have earned your forgiveness, for not having the time to find another to do this work. Now that I have you excited about what you will find as you read, let me close and permit you to begin enjoying the amazing realities obtainable in choosing to use our gift of faith.

CHAPTER 1

Why Me?

My story is one of a man called by God to do His work, who for decades was the biggest failure of all time. It is a living testimony to the faithfulness, forgiveness, and perfect love of God. Its main element is using the wonderful gift of faith, which God gives to everyone coming into this world.

The title I picked for the opening chapter might relate you to questioning God as to why I had so many different serious illnesses trying to destroy my body. But that is not really what I mean to imply. "Why me?" refers to my difficulty in understanding why God would pick someone so unworthy, to be used by Him. I have been one of the most horrible of sinners. For having heard God calling me to His ministry since a little boy, hiking in the hills of my Kentucky home, then having become born again in 1974, hearing the Holy Spirit telling me, "I've given you what you said you lacked. Now go and do My work." I spent decades running away from His call.

We were approaching the new millennium, and I was managing a retail store in Tyrone Square Mall. One day, I received a serious message of warning from the Holy Spirit. "Joe, do you realize you are on your way to spending your eternity among the poorest of souls in heaven?" Naturally this shocked me, so I asked why. "Because for decades you have run away from My call to use you for My honor and glory."

I knew at once this was true, and I was more than guilty. I had allowed pursuit of the world and the things it had to offer, interfering with God's plan for my life. Guilty as charged! What a frightening thought. What could I do? What must I do? Fortunately, being familiar with God's love and His word, I knew at once the answer. I must ask for forgiveness and seek with all of my might, for the Holy Spirit to help me turn things around.

Repentance became my daily goal, not just repentance but sincere and heartfelt sorrow over having for decades been such a miserable failure to my Lord. I daily prayed my heart out to the Lord, asking for His forgiveness and promising, if given the chance, I would try my best not to remain a failure to Him. One day, after having spent at least a year praying as I did, it occurred to me; I need much more than "my best," if I were to succeed in being used mightily by God. I needed the messages I would be sharing to come only from the anointing of the Holy Spirit.

In taking an appraisal of me, my ability to fail God, and my wondering why God would choose someone like me (I knew if I were God, someone like me would be my very last choice), I discovered something fascinating. I found I was much like St. Paul. St. Paul called himself chief of sinners. He knew any ability he had been given to lead others to Jesus came from the anointing of the Holy Spirit at work in his life and not from him.

Realizing the similarities, I understood how I would easily be among the chief of sinners of my generation. I knew also, if I were to be an effective minister of the Gospel, what I teach and say must come from the Spirit of Truth and Him only. Now the chief of sinners is not an enviable title to pursue. It also is a hard one to live down. Nevertheless, I knew as God had answered Paul's desire to turn his life around, He would do so for me too, if I only asked and *believed* He would.

This now became my daily prayer. "Father God, please help me to be like St. Paul. Turn my life around and help me to be used mightily for

Your honor and glory, before I must die. It is still an uphill battle. satan comes against me like never before, and to be honest, sometimes I still lose a battle or two. But I have learned to place my failures under the blood of Jesus and continue each new day to fight the good fight."

Is satan thrilled? You need only to read till the end, this true accounting of all my Heavenly Father has delivered me from to know the answer.

It is my prayer that when you have finished, if you have yet to surrender your sins and your heart to Jesus, asking Him to become your Lord and Savior, you will without delay. Also, if you have let satan try to get away with stealing your gift of faith, given you at birth by your Heavenly Father, you will put a quick end to satan's plans. If you have as yet to use your gift of faith to help lead you to the one true God, may you do so now. Please do not miss out another day on enjoying the deep and loving relationship (not religion) which Jesus came to restore between our Father and we, His creation.

Now, *fasten your seat belt*! Listen to my true story of God's mercy, love, and grace applied to the life of a sinner.

CHAPTER 2

It All Began with Severe Headaches

It was June of 2013 that I started having severe headaches. I'm one who rarely gets a headache. Even when I do, usually it is mild, and an aspirin makes it go away. But not so this time. I tried over-the-counter reliefs and much prayer, asking my pastor to lay his hands on my forehead and seeking healing from God. But nothing seemed to stop the excessive pain I was feeling daily. I decided to go to the VA and check in, to see if they could find the cause and cure for these migraine-like headaches.

I spent a total of four days in the hospital. During this time, CT scans and PET scans were taken. I also had a very bad occurrence with delusions. I believed they were holding me against my will, tying to brainwash me, and even had threatened the life of my sister. I was angry enough to go to war. You can threaten my life; I can deal with it. But threaten the life of my sister, you'll have to answer to my fist.

Fortunately, I was far too weak to engage in physical fighting. I did, however, once try to escape. These delusions were so real. It was like being in a color 3-D movie. Every actor played their part to perfection, and the script fit the imagined scenario to perfection. It was one of the strangest things I've ever encountered. It was clear satan was involved, as I found myself using foul mouth-cussing words, sometimes even adding in God's name. Vulgarity, which all of my life I had avoided like the plague, began to come from my mouth. It was a nightmare!

I was put into a room which had four other delusional patients. Some of them had far worse experiences than me. They would scream and cry out in the middle of the night. In the 1960s there was a movie called *The Snake Pit*. It was about a sane woman being placed inside of an insane asylum. Being in that environment for a length of time made her begin to take on the characteristics of the insane. This was close to what it was like for me.

Then, as I began to regain my ability to think clearly, I knew that in order for me to maintain my sanity, I must enter into spiritual warfare. So, whenever the idea of cussing and using vulgarity started to try coming from my mouth, I would shout out saying, "Lord, in You do I live and breathe and move and have my being!" satan would flee! I would be shouting this in the wee hours of the morning, as the other patients were shouting their remarks. Surely, the nurse on duty must have thought I was as far out as the others. But I knew I was in spiritual combat with demons that wanted to take control of my mind and tongue. When you are in a situation like that, it is so wonderful to have the Comforter within to call on.

On the fourth day, a battery of four doctors came into my room to interview me. One was the chief of the psychology department, another was the chief of the oncology department, and still another was the chief of the whole hospital. The fourth was in charge of my treatment. Each asked me a series of questions, ranging from my name, how old I was, and what day and date it was. I guess I must have passed, because they arranged for my release later that day. But sadly, late into that day, I was still using cuss words I *never* believed in using before. I prayed sincerely asking of God to never permit me to become under the influence of such delusions again.

I was given an appointment to come back to see the head oncologist in three days. When I did, he revealed to me what had happened to cause me to become so delusional. It was discovered by the use of the scans that I had several cancerous lesions on my liver. They had caused a spike in my calcium rate, which triggered the delusions. The doctor, who was a very kind and considerate man, then told me of his plan of attack. First, we are going to take a biopsy, to learn just what kind of cancer it is. Then we will know what kind of chemotherapy we must use to treat it.

At this piece of news, I very abruptly said, "No you're not!"

The poor doctor looked at me puzzled and asked, "What do you plan on doing? Just dying?"

Laughingly I said, "No! I plan on living! I'm going to do the *best* possible thing I can do."

"What is that?" The doctor asked.

"I'm going to use my gift of faith in my Father's perfect love for me, then trust in His will to be done in my life. I have work to do for God, and I don't think it's time for me to go just yet."

At this, the doctor told me he wished me luck. I said luck has nothing to do with it. I explained that because of the sacrifice of love made for me on the cross by my savior, Jesus, God's Son, I now have my relationship with my Heavenly Father restored. My body has become a temple of God's Holy Spirit, and I can even go boldly before Him in His throne room and make my petitions known to Him.

It now has been over several years. I keep telling myself I must go back and see this doctor once more and show him the power of faith in the one true God.

Can you believe it? This is only the start of a great and wonderful adventure! Please read on for more good news.

CHAPTER 3

The Power and Fun of Being a Witness for God

This first encounter with the oncologist was in the morning. Later that afternoon, I was scheduled to see my primary physician, Dr. K. She is a lovely young lady from India, professing the Hindu faith.

The first thing Dr. K. said to me was, "I suppose you have already heard the news? They found numerous cancerous lesions on your liver."

To which I calmly replied, "Yes, Dr. M. told me that earlier. It's no big thing."

At my calmness and my answer, Dr. K. had the same look of amazement on her face, as did Dr. M. Noting this, I looked at her and said, "I can see you have the same look of amazement on your face as Dr. M. did." (The look was as if thinking, "I just said you have cancer. Why aren't you afraid? Don't you know the meaning of that disease, and what it can do to your body?")

So I think I'd better explain. "I believe both you and Dr. M. have seen far too many 'religious Christians.' Those whom once you said the word cancer, fell off the chair, and began to lay on the floor, sucking their thumb, and pounding the floor, all the while crying and saying in fear, 'I've got cancer. I'm going to die!'"

As I was sharing this scenario, Dr. K. looked at me nodding her head in agreement. When I finished, I said, "Thankfully I was delivered from religion many years ago. I now have relationship with my Father in heaven. I know His love for me is perfect, and His plan for my life will be fulfilled. I trust in Him, more than I do doctors or chemotherapy."

Having been told I had refused chemo treatment, it was agreed I would come back every three months for a blood test, to see how I was doing. The days went by quickly, and suddenly, it was time for my first blood test results. I went to see Dr. K. and was told things looked the same.

Dr. K. and the Death Sentence

Before the next blood test results were due, I experienced what could be perceived as alarming symptoms. I began to become very weak in my body. My walking began to resemble that of Tim Conway's "little old man," barely one foot in front of another. I was not happy with this. But my faith in God remained firm that it was only a test, and I would recover.

Arriving at Dr. K.'s exam room, she had a grim look on her face. Dr. K. had made a copy of my blood test to attempt to explain my problem. On the chart, she had used a yellow marker to trace the two lines which ran off the chart.

Looking at me with a sad look on her face, Dr. K. announced to me, "I'm very sorry to have to tell you this, Mr. Callihan. But your latest blood test reveal you have only two to three weeks left to live."

"Really?" I questioned.

At this, Dr. K. showed the copy of the chart and, using her pen, proceeded to follow the two lines up and off the chart. One represented my calcium count; I can't remember what the other represented. "When this is high and this is also high, it means you have little time to live. As you can see, both of yours are off the chart! So I would suggest you allow me to arrange to place you in hospice for the remaining time."

I replied by saying, "I can see where you're coming from. In medical school, they teach you that if this is high and this is high, the next step is death. Am I right?" At this, she nodded her head in agreement. What peace and joy flooded within my spirit, as with a big grin I said, "I've got good news for you, Dr. K. I don't live by sight. I live by faith. One thing I can guarantee is no two lines on a piece of paper will determine if, when, and how I die. Only my Heavenly Father, God Almighty, has that authority. You can show me charts all day, and I will not be afraid. So I must say thanks, but no thanks to your offer of hospice care."

At this, Dr. K. became angry. She tried not showing it on her face. But it was reflected in the tone of her voice, she said, "I was going to have you come back and see me in two weeks. Why don't we make it three months?"

I replied, "That's fine with me!"

The Next Visit

Again, those three months went by quickly. During that time, my energy and strength was restored to me. I was once more walking with a healthy stride. Here's the fun part. I walked into Dr. K.'s examining room smiling. With a happy voice, I announced my presence.

"Hi Dr. K., how are you doing? As you can see, I'm doing *great!*"

The look on her face was priceless. It was like what you see in the movies and on sitcoms. Her mouth dropped open; she stared at me, with a speechless look. You could almost read her mind. (What are you doing here? You're supposed to be outside, buried in the cemetery.) Note, the VA cemetery is located just about a block away from where we were.

A high calcium count can cause you to become delusional. As previously reported that actually happened to me when I spent the four days in the VA hospital in July 2013. I thought the people at the VA wanted to kidnap and brainwash me. Fortunately, I knew I was far too weak to take them on in physical warfare. So that was out. However, once I did try to escape, wearing only my gown. I almost made it out into the public. They stopped me just in time.

So, on one of my visits to see Dr. K., I was informed that my calcium count had risen way too high. In fact, I was nearing delusion mode. It was suggested that I spend some time in the hospital getting intravenous treatment which brought the calcium down. It was on a Wednesday. I checked in the same day I had spoken with Dr. K. She arranged for my immediate entry to the hospital.

There was just one small problem, one which I had made Dr. K. aware of. Joanne Derstine, daughter of Gerald Derstine, founder of Christian Retreat, had asked me to be a guest speaker at one of her Writer's Conferences, which is held at the beautiful Christian Retreat in Bradenton, Florida. My topic was to be, "How to get self-published." I was due to speak on Saturday. Dr. K. had made me realize the last thing I needed was to go there, become delirious, and go around accusing them of trying to kidnap and brainwash me. I could see myself speaking from the podium and fearfully saying I needed to escape. Can you imagine what kind of embarrassing comedy that would have been?

Nevertheless, when Friday came around, in the afternoon I was informed my calcium count had not as yet gone down enough and I would need to stay another day (which would be Saturday). I knew I had a decision to make. I realized satan wanted me not to attend the conference. I was advised surely, they'll understand if you cancel out at the last moment. So I spoke with God about it and decided to go anyway and make satan cry. I had to sign myself out, with the understanding if anything harmful happened, the VA would not be held responsible for it. This I did without any worry, anxiety, or concerns. As you may have guessed, all went well.

Here I go again. I almost forgot to tell you. This time, when Dr. K. was urging me not to go to the conference but check into the hospital immediately, she did something which moved my heart. After warning me repeatedly that if I were to attempt to go with my present condition, I most likely would not come back alive. I kept on assuring her with God's help; I would be OK. Then, with tears in her eyes, she hugged me and said, "If you were to die, I would miss you. You are a good man." That is what it did for me. That was why I agreed to stay in the hospital until late Friday. It was a compromise.

Is this going to make a great book or what?
Every day walking with God leads to adventure!

CHAPTER 4

Getting a Second Opinion

As you well know, when given a diagnosis of cancer, the thing to do is to get a second opinion. This is what I did, about six months after having been told by the VA doctors that I had cancerous lesions on my liver. Using my Medicare benefit, I sought out an insurance company and became a patient of one of their doctors.

At Dr. Fana's, I was assigned to Dr. B. to be my personal physician. In explaining the results, I was told the CT and PET scans at the VA had revealed cancerous lesions and of my choice to use my faith over chemo. Dr. B. arranged for me to have X-rays taken, to see if there was any trace of cancer in my body.

I lost count; they must have taken at least twenty X-rays, sides, front and back, etc. When I went back to see Dr. B. to get the results, he showed me on his cell phone the report which had been sent to him. They had found no evidence of tumors anywhere on my body. They had however discovered that I now had multiple myeloma, which is a blood cancer. Dr. B. suggested I visit their oncologist, Dr. A. He would do a biopsy and determine if it had gotten into my bones. I agreed this would be a wise choice.

I followed through and was told the myeloma had not "yet" gotten inside of my bones. It was here that Dr. A. suggested I agree to have administered intravenously, a new drug. It was not chemo, and it only destroyed the myeloma, not attacking or harming any innocent tissue or organs. You like to trust your doctor as an honest person. So, based on what I had been told, I agreed to proceed with this treatment. It was to be twice a week, costing $80.00 per session. When I asked for how long, the answer I received was for however long it takes to get rid of the myeloma.

Thank God I am not completely dumb nor totally trusting. So I asked Dr. A. to give me the name of this drug he would be using. I even asked that he spell it out on a piece of paper for me. He did, and when I got home, I cranked up the computer, seeking information about this new wonder drug. In doing so, I discovered that Dr. A. had (as

Hillary Clinton is prone to do) "misspoken." It turns out that he had deliberately "fibbed" to me about this treatment. It was just another form of chemo.

The information I found said it was a chemo treatment. It had possible side effects such as kidney failure, heart attack, stroke, or blindness to offer. Also, although a five-year life expectancy was normal, among the "elderly," it was only two years. Now approaching my seventies, although a young man lives inside of me, I thought technically, I might be considered among the "elderly." I thought to myself, "What is two years, compared to the number of years God might have in mind for me to live?"

The day arrived for me to start the treatment. I said to Dr. A., "If you don't mind, I will forgo the treatment you have in mind. I'd rather put my faith in God, as I've done thus far."

Dr. A. then began to extol the virtues of the drug.

I replied, "Are you aware of the many wonderful side effects it has to offer, blindness, kidney failure, heart attack, stroke? I don't want or need any of that. Father God only wants what is good for my body. It's the temple of His Holy Spirit. He would never give me any of what this chemo has to offer. So no, thank you. I'll stay with God."

Dr. A. then tried selling me on the same line they use to reassure Christian people it's OK to go with chemo.

He said, "You have to remember. It's God who gives man the ability to come up with such life—saving drugs."

I replied, "If God is in it, why would it be able to cause the remainder of your life to become a living nightmare? You can believe that, if you want. But I know my Heavenly Father too well to swallow that lie."

Dr. A. spoke with me for quite a while regarding my need for this treatment. He even went so far as to assure me I would be facing eminent death in refusing. (See the following, from his notes.) Dr. A. told me, as a fellow Christian, he understood where I was coming from. But as a doctor, he had to tell me what I wanted to do is unsound. He assured me if I did not take the chemo, I most likely would not live out the year. (This was in 2014).

TESTIMONY OF A MIRACLE MAN

5/29/14
LAST VISIT

Radiology Reports

Print?	Date of Doc.	Name	MD Interpretation	Comment
☐	4/14/2014	Skeletal Survey	POD	Two lytic lesions involving the frontal calvarium vertex along with a lytic lesion involving the proximal left femur.
☐	4/14/2014	Ultrasound Abdomen	Stable	Diffuse hydrogenous echo texture of the liver parenchyma without liver lesions. Mild splenomegaly with 2 hyperechoic nodules within the spleen measuring 1.3 and 0.9 cm of uncertain etiology.

IMPRESSION

5/8/14
PATIENT BONE MARROW DOES NOT HAVE ANY PLASMACYTOSIS. NO SERUM MONOCLONAL GAMMOPATHY. HOWEVER HE HAD AND HAS ELEVATED CALCIUM, CKD, ELEVATED IgA, ELEVATED SERUM KAPPA/LAMBDA LIGHT CHAINS THOUGH WITH NORMAL RATIO, ELEVATED B2M AND LYTIC LESIONS.
I SUSPECT HE HAS NON-SECRETORY MYELOMA OR LIGHT CHAIN MYELOMA.

WILL CHECK 24 HRS. UPEP WITH IMMUNOFIXATION ALONG WITH REPEAT TESTING FOR OTHER PARAMETERS AS BELOW.

5/22/14
PATIENT AGAIN HAS VERY HIGH CALCIUM, GOING UP FROM 10.7 TO 11.9. CONSIDERING HIS RECENT ADMISSION TO VAMC WITH DELIRIUM AND HYPERCALCEMIA AND LONG WEEKEND COMING UP WILL GIVE RENALLY ADJUSTED DOSE OF AREDIA TOMORROW.
PATIENT WILL NEED XGEVA TREATMENT FOR LYTIC BONE DISEASE AS HIS RENAL FUNCTION IS MARGINAL FOR IV BISPHOSPHONATES.
WILL ALSO NEED VELCADE + DECADRON FOR NON-SECRETORY MYELOMA.
DISCUSSED DRUGS, THEIR SIDE EFFECTS, RR,MS,OS AS WELL AS COMPLICATIONS. HE VERBALIZES UNDERSTANDING

/29/14
TOLERATED AREDIA WELL WITH CALCIUM DECREASE
DISCUSSED VELCADE, ITS RR,MS,OS AS WELL AS TOXICITIES AND SUPPORTIVE CARE.

PATIENT IS REFUSING ALL TREATMENTS INCLUDING VELCADE, XGEVA, DECADRON OR ANY SUPPORTIVE CARE. HE TELLS ME THAT HE HAS READ AND TALKED TO HIS FRIENDS AND FAMILY AND IS MAKING A INFORMED DECISION.

I TOLD HIM THAT HE HAS AGRESSIVE DISEASE AND THE TREATMENT IS GENERALLY VERY TOLERABLE WITH GOAL TO PREVENT MORBIDITY, IMPROVE OR MAINTAIN QOL AND HOPEFULLY AS PER DATA IMPROVE OS.

HE IS ADAMANT THAT HE DOES NOT WANT TREATMENT AND THAT " HIS GOD AND PRAYERS WILL HEAL THE DISEASE JUST LIKE IN THE PAST HIS LIVER LESIONS WERE HEALED BY PRAYERS"
I HAD A LONG DISCUSSION WITH PATIENT OF MORE THAN 30-40 MINUTES DISCUSSING ALL THE RISKS, COMPLICATIONS AS WELL AS EARLY DEATH THAT COULD ENSUE FROM DISEASE PROGRESSION. HE REMAINS FIRM ON HIS BELIEFS. I RESPECT HIS WISHES AND TOLD HIM THAT I'M AVAILABLE TO DISCUSS THIS ISSUE FURTHER AND WILL BE HAPPY TO TAKE CARE OF HIM WITH OR WITH OUT TREATMENT.

IN THE MEANTIME HE WILL FOLLOW UP WITH DR. B█████ AND WITH ME IF NEEDED.

RECOMMENDATIONS and PLAN
FOLLOW UP WITH DR. B█████ AND WITH ME AS NEEDED.
PATIENT REFUSES ALL TREATMENT.

CHAPTER 5

New Doctors Arrive on the Scene

It was in mid-December of 2014 that Dr. K. informed me she was leaving the VA to pursue work in medical research. This was a sad time for both of us. Dr. K. is a very caring doctor. She truly cares about the well-being of every patient. I had even once warned her about this, telling how it could lead to becoming burnt out. In the course of our association, she had witnessed how the one true God had worked medical wonders in my body.

At this point, I must tell you that I was under the care of my outside doctor, Dr. B. Every two months, he was giving me intravenously two bags of saline solution. It was used to bring down the high calcium count, which could cause delusions. Every two months, the count would rise again to a dangerous high. Then the saline was administered to keep it in check.

I say this because in her parting words to me, Dr. K. issued a warning. "You realize the saline solution you are using is only delaying the inevitable. If ever you stop, first, you will become very weak. Then you will become delusional. Lastly, you will die."

I thanked her for all of the great help she had been to me over the time I had been her patient. I offered her God's blessings, as we said goodbye.

As I said, that was in mid-December of 2014. In January of 2015, upon my appointment to see Dr. B. once more, I was greeted by Dr. Fana, the head doctor. He informed me Dr. B. was no longer at his practice. He had moved, to be closer to where he lived.

Dr. Fana said to me, "I'll be taking you on as my patient." Then he said, "I see where you are dealing with multiple myeloma. I'll make an appointment for you to see Dr. A., our oncologist, and he can give you chemo treatment to fight it."

I replied with, "Been there, done that, and it's not going to happen."

With a surprised look on his face, I proceeded to tell Dr. Fana of my visit with Dr. A. and of my faith in my God and Father. He agreed with me. But then said, "I see you've been taking saline solutions to keep your calcium count down. I'm going to stop those infusions. I'll give it to you today, because I see your count is too high. But this will be the last time."

I just smiled and said, "That's fine with me."

On my way driving home, I spoke with Father God and said, "Well, Lord, it looks like it's going to be really just You and me, not even salt water in my veins. But that's what faith is about anyway, isn't it?" I knew my sense of humor must have given Father God a good laugh; it did me.

I got to visit Dr. Fana again in April. On this visit, he said, "I see your calcium count is up too high again. So I'm going to give you the saline but for the last time." And it was!

In May of 2015, I got to meet for the first time, my newly assigned PC doctor at the VA. His name being difficult for some to pronounce, he just goes by the name of Dr. Z. On this, my first visit, he questioned me about my medical history. As I reported the adventures I had been encountering with the reports of cancer, he followed by looking at the reports on the computer screen. He said he admired my faith in God and would not offer me any chemo treatments. (See progress notes below.)

Again, on June 15, 2015, in his progress report, Dr. Z. confirmed all of the maladies I was facing. Here is what he put into his report, "Assessment: Dx this patient by history of multiple myeloma with hypercalcemia on intermittent outside medical follow-up with hydration of normal saline mitigate hypercalcemia with significant interval stopping of treatment and without adverse symptomatology.

Plan: Patient is electing to continue his strong treatment by faith. Significant interval improvement in numbers including creatinine PSA. Close outpatient monitoring to continue, along with support on the outside, as per patient's directives."

JOSEPH CALLIHAN

Progress Notes

Printed On May 19,

```
Measurement DT    WEIGHT
                  LB(KG)[BMI]

05/12/2015 10:27  186(84.37)[27]
BMI 27.1
Weight last read May 12, 2015@10:27:32
Height last read May 12, 2015@10:27:32
```

Physical exam

Integument	tone turgor within normal limits WNL, no ecchymoses, old scars, Photodermatitis
HEENT	normocephalic, atraumatic, symmetrical, PERRLA, conjunctiva pink WNL
	TM WNL cerumen, nasopharynx, no significant erythema or congestion,
	No bruits of significance, R to L equal, no asymmetry noted
RESP e	BS+ right to left equal, no wheezing, no rubs, air entry with good expansion, no effusions, no sign of labored breathing at rest
COR	Heart NSR with no murmur, rub, gallop, heave, or lift no ectopy
ABD	Abdomen benign without masses or organomegaly no significant tendern
EXT	no clubbing or cyanosis, no malrotation, no edema, trace
CNS	no focality, R TO L equal and symmetrical, DTR symmetrical and equal
	No obvious deficits, no evidence of muscle wasting, cranial nerves WNL no noted tonicoclonic activity, no asterixis
Rectal	deferred.

Assessment: Dx patient's diagnosis is consistent with hypercalcemia of malignancy possible multiple myeloma coronary artery disease status post coronary artery bypass graft hypertension with resolution of his diabetes

Plan: Per patient's request in view of his strong faith and believes routine followup in 3 months with blood work requested continued monitoring ongoing

Patient to call or return if questions or concerns.

Healthy lifestyle encouraged including no smoking, minimal alcohol use, weight control and regular exercise as tolerated for age and condition. Maintain compliance with medications.

Item Ordered	START DATE	STOP DATE	ENTERED
DIABETIC NEPHROPATHY S	MAY 12, 2015		MAY 12, 2015@11:01

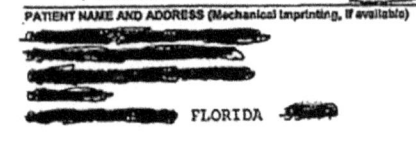

VISTA Electronic Medical Documentation
Printed at CW BILL YOUNG VAMC

FLORIDA

TESTIMONY OF A MIRACLE MAN

Progress Notes
WRITER Printed On May 19, 20'

alcohol no exposure to toxins he currently is a right or he has been a courier within the Navy without exposure to toxins in the Panama Canal zone

Patient's mom passed away in her 70s in association with complications of alcohol in addition patient's father passed away in his 80s of unknown etiology he does have a half-brother and 2 half-sisters reportedly healthy and has no children he is a widower from a late marriage in his 60s

ALLERGIES: CHEESE, DEFINITY 2ML, OPTISON

Active Outpatient Medications (including Supplies):

	Active Non-VA Medications	Refills	Start Date Expiration
1)	Non-VA FOLIC ACID 0.4MG TAB Sig: 0.8 MG MOUTH EVERY DAY	ACTIVE	
2)	Non-VA METOPROLOL (TARTRATE) 50MG TAB Sig: 50MG MOUTH TWICE A DAY	ACTIVE	
3)	Non-VA MULTIVITAMIN/MINERALS THERAPEUT CAP/TAB Sig: 1 TABLET MOUTH DAILY	ACTIVE	
4)	Non-VA NO NON-VA DRUGS, HERBALS OR OTC'S Sig: PER PATIENT INTERVIEW	ACTIVE	
5)	Non-VA POTASSIUM CHLORIDE 20MEQ SA TAB Sig: 20MEQ MOUTH EVERY DAY	ACTIVE	
6)	Non-VA RED YEAST RICE CAP/TAB Sig: MOUTH DAILY	ACTIVE	
7)	Non-VA SAW PALMETTO CAP/TAB Sig:	ACTIVE	

Past Medical History unchanged since last visit

Review of Systems:
Patient denies any positive findings he does admit to nocturia x3 occasionally Negative for other organ system issues today

Vital signs
BP:129/65 (05/12/2015 10:27)
Pain:0 (05/12/2015 10:27)
Pulse:49 (05/12/2015 10:27)
RR:18 (05/12/2015 10:27)
Temp:98.1 F [36.7 C] (05/12/2015 10:27)
Pulse ox: SVS - Vital Signs Selected (max 1 occurrence or 30 days)
  No data available for PULSE OXIMETRY
99 (L/MIN)(%) (12/18/2014 12:34)
SVS - WEIGHT WITHIN 30 D (max 1 occurrence or 30 days)

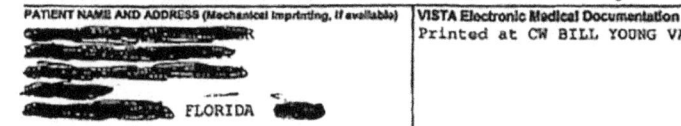

PATIENT NAME AND ADDRESS (Mechanical Imprinting, if available) | VISTA Electronic Medical Documentation
Printed at CW BILL YOUNG VAMC

FLORIDA

JOSEPH CALLIHAN

Progress Notes

Printed On May 19, 2015

```
LOCAL TITLE: PRIMARY CARE MEDICINE
STANDARD TITLE: PRIMARY CARE PHYSICIAN NOTE
DATE OF NOTE: MAY 12, 2015@10:56     ENTRY DATE: MAY 12, 2015@10:56:20
      AUTHOR: ZAHAROWITZ, HERMAN    EXP COSIGNER:
     URGENCY:                            STATUS: COMPLETED
```

FOLLOW UP VISIT: MAY 12, 2015

CALLIHAN, JOSEPH BEECHER   (727) 723-5631

Age: 71
186 lb [84.5 kg] (05/12/2015 10:27)   69.5 in [176.5 cm] (05/12/2015 10:27)
BMI 27.1
Weight last read May 12, 2015@10:27:32
Height last read May 12, 2015@10:27:32

BP: 129/65 (05/12/2015 10:27) Pulse: 49 (05/12/2015 10:27)

Office visit: Patient is a 71-year-old gentleman who returns for routine medical evaluation and followup

Patient has an extremely strong faith in God as a result of which his history includes multiple medical events with lab evidence in followup but he has been able to skirt and avoid presenting alert oriented functional and in good spirits

Patient's prior history includes but is not limited to having had hypercalcemia at 10.5 associated with malignancy multiple myeloma with protein spike renal failure with creatinine of 2.46 hypertension obesity with weight now reduced from 265 pounds to 165 and back up to his present weight of 185 he does report hyperlipidemia hiatal hernia gastroesophageal reflux disease and coronary artery bypass graft for which he has a scar

Patient was also noted to have diabetes with elevations of hemoglobin A1c in the sevens however currently he is perfectly normal with hemoglobin A1c around 5

Patient was found to have renal tumors which apparently were self-limited and resolved within a six-month period CT and PET scan confirmed the above including there is a *SERIES OF X-RAYS CONFIRMING TUMORS NO LONGER PRESENT WITHIN PATIENT'S BODY.*

Labs: discussed lab findings discussed patient's calcium was noted to have been as high as 10.5 creatinine renal failure as high as 2.46 M protein spikes consistent with possible myeloma in the past

Social History: Patient is originally from Kentucky there is no smoking or

---

PATIENT NAME AND ADDRESS (Mechanical Imprinting, if available) | VISTA Electronic Medical Documentation
CALLIHAN, JOSEPH BEECHER | Printed at CW BILL YOUNG VAMC
▬▬▬▬▬▬▬▬▬▬
▬▬▬▬▬▬▬▬, FLORIDA ▬▬▬

Page 3

TESTIMONY OF A MIRACLE MAN

Progress Notes

Printed On Jun 15, 2016

```
LOCAL TITLE: PRIMARY CARE MEDICINE
STANDARD TITLE: PRIMARY CARE PHYSICIAN NOTE
DATE OF NOTE: MAY 23, 2016@11:33     ENTRY DATE: MAY 23, 2016@11:33:19
     AUTHOR: Z.                      EXP COSIGNER:
    URGENCY:                             STATUS: COMPLETED
```

FOLLOW UP VISIT: MAY 23, 2016

CALLIHAN, JOSEPH BEECHER

Age: 72
213 lb [96.8 kg] (05/23/2016 10:21)   69.5 in [176.5 cm] (05/23/2016 10:21)
BMI 31.1
Weight last read May 23, 2016@10:21:13
Height last read May 23, 2016@10:21:13

BP:143/85 (05/23/2016 10:24) Pulse: 82 (05/23/2016 10:21)

Office visit: Patient returns to clinic complaining of gastroesophageal reflux he seems to be indulging in sweets on occasion and that may or may not have a direct relationship he also has urinary tract symptoms and he was noted to have kidney failure with a rise from 3.38-3.14 in association with multiple myeloma and hypercalcemia

Labs: discussed patient is noted with pyuria his creatinine continues to rise currently at 3.29 he also has PSA elevation of 6.6 hypercalcemia significant at 10.9 patient's total cholesterol HDL risk is 4.8 thrombocytopenia 101,000 with anemia of 11.9

Social History: Patient reports little social history change please see prior note February 22, 2016 for detail in regards to social history family history or any review of system interval changes

ALLERGIES: CHEESE, DEFINITY 2ML, OPTISON

Active Outpatient Medications (including Supplies):

	Active Outpatient Medications	Status Refills	Issue Date Last Fill Expiration
1)	DEXTRAN 70/HYPROMELLOSE 0.3% SOL 0.9ML Qty: 72 for 30 days Sig: INSTILL 1 DROP IN EACH EYE FOUR TIMES A DAY FOR	ACTIVE Refills: 4	Issu:02-22-16 Last:02-24-16 Expr:02-22-17

PATIENT NAME AND ADDRESS (Mechanical Imprinting, if available)
CALLIHAN, JOSEPH BEECHER

FLORIDA

VISTA Electronic Medical Documentation
Printed at C.W. BILL YOUNG DEPT OF VAMC

Page 1

JOSEPH CALLIHAN

Progress Notes

Printed On Jun 15, 2016

EYES

```
                                                          Start Date
    Active Non-VA Medications              Refills        Expiration
    ===============================================================
1)  Non-VA FOLIC ACID 0.4MG TAB   Sig: 0.8 MG    ACTIVE
       MOUTH EVERY DAY
2)  Non-VA METOPROLOL (TARTRATE) 50MG TAB        ACTIVE
       Sig: 50MG MOUTH TWICE A DAY
3)  Non-VA MULTIVITAMIN/MINERALS THERAPEUT       ACTIVE
       CAP/TAB  Sig: 1 TABLET MOUTH DAILY
4)  Non-VA NO NON-VA DRUGS, HERBALS OR OTC'S     ACTIVE
       Sig: PER PATIENT INTERVIEW
5)  Non-VA POTASSIUM CHLORIDE 20MEQ SA TAB       ACTIVE
       Sig: 20MEQ MOUTH EVERY DAY
6)  Non-VA RED YEAST RICE CAP/TAB  Sig:          ACTIVE
       MOUTH DAILY
7)  Non-VA SAW PALMETTO CAP/TAB  Sig:            ACTIVE
```

8 Total Medications

Past Medical History unchanged since last visit

Review of Systems: Patient reports UTI symptoms he does have pyuria both significant heme and white cell count in addition he complains of gastroesophageal reflux self discontinued proton blocker after the news of its effects but were not desirable reason for which he self discontinued them all 10 other systems are otherwise noncontributory
 Negative for other organ system issues today

Vital signs
BP:143/85 (05/23/2016 10:24)
Pain:0 (05/23/2016 10:21)
Pulse:82 (05/23/2016 10:21)
RR:18 (05/23/2016 10:21)
Temp:97.6 F [36.4 C] (05/23/2016 10:21)
Pulse ox: SVS - Vital Signs Selected (max 1 occurrence or 30 days)
  No data available for PULSE OXIMETRY
99 (L/MIN)(%) (12/18/2014 12:34)
SVS - WEIGHT WITHIN 30 D (max 1 occurrence or 30 days)
Measurement DT   WEIGHT
                   LB(KG)[BMI]

05/23/2016 10:21   213(96.62)(31*)
BMI 31.1
Weight last read May 23, 2016@10:21:13
Height last read May 23, 2016@10:21:13

PATIENT NAME AND ADDRESS (Mechanical Imprinting, if available) | VISTA Electronic Medical Documentation
CALLIHAN, JOSEPH BEECHER | Printed at C.W. BILL YOUNG DEPT OF VAMC

FLORIDA

TESTIMONY OF A MIRACLE MAN

Progress Notes

Printed On Jun 15, 2016

Physical exam

Integument	tone turgor within normal limits WNL, no ecchymoses, old scars, Photodermatitis
HEENT	normocephalic, atraumatic, symmetrical, PERRLA, conjunctiva pink WNL TM WNL cerumen, nasopharynx, no significant erythema or congestion, No bruits of significance, R to L equal, no asymmetry noted
RESP e	BS+ right to left equal, no wheezing, no rubs, air entry with good expansion, no effusions, no sign of labored breathing at rest
COR	Heart NSR with no murmur, rub, gallop, heave, or lift no ectopy
ABD	Abdomen benign without masses or organomegaly no significant tendern
EXT	no clubbing or cyanosis, no malrotation, no edema, trace
CNS	no focality, R TO L equal and symmetrical, DTR symmetrical and equal No obvious deficits, no evidence of muscle wasting, cranial nerves WNL no noted tonicoclonic activity, no asterixis
Rectal	deferred.

Assessment: Dx progressive renal failure now with a creatinine up to 3.29 multiple myeloma with significant hypercalcemia calcium of 10.9 obstructive uropathy of the prostate with PSA of 6.6 uric acid of 9.2 total cholesterol HDL risk of 4.8 thrombocytopenia of 100 or 1000 with anemia of hemoglobin 11.9 mult myelo

Patient referred to urology alternatives to gastroesophageal reflux with TUMS after cessation of proton inhibitor by patient GU to adverse news associated Rx

Patient referred to urology clinic for further followup to rule out any obstruction or mass or kidney stone encouraged hydration and antibiotics initiated

Plan: Return to clinic her regularly scheduled visits with pre-appointment lab work as usual patient continues to follow this contents on choosing treatment modalities appropriate for his care with strong faith

Patient to call or return if questions or concerns.

Healthy lifestyle encouraged including no smoking, minimal alcohol use, weight control and regular exercise as tolerated for age and condition. Maintain compliance with medications.

Item Ordered	START DATE	STOP DATE	ENTERED
CIPROFLOXACIN TAB			MAY 23, 2016@11:41
OCCULT BLOOD FIT X1 SC	MAY 23, 2016		MAY 23, 2016@10:24

PATIENT NAME AND ADDRESS (Mechanical Imprinting, if available)
CALLIHAN, JOSEPH BEECHER

FLORIDA

VISTA Electronic Medical Documentation
Printed at C.W. BILL YOUNG DEPT OF VAMC

Page 3

JOSEPH CALLIHAN

Progress Notes

Printed On Aug 19, 2015

LOCAL TITLE: PRIMARY CARE MEDICINE
STANDARD TITLE: PRIMARY CARE PHYSICIAN NOTE
DATE OF NOTE: AUG 17, 2015@11:19   ENTRY DATE: AUG 17, 2015@11:19:51
    AUTHOR: Z████████████   EXP COSIGNER:
    URGENCY: STATUS: COMPLETED

FOLLOW UP VISIT: AUG 17, 2015

CALLIHAN, JOSEPH BEECHER ████████

Age: 71
194 lb [88.2 kg] (08/17/2015 10:25)   69 in (175.3 cm) (08/17/2015 10:25)
BMI 28.7
Weight last read Aug 17, 2015@10:25:14
Height last read Aug 17, 2015@10:25:14

BP:134/77 (08/17/2015 10:25) Pulse: 52 (08/17/2015 10:25)

Office visit: Patient is a 1-year-old gentleman who returns for followup, he has strong faith in God as a result of which he has declined interventional treatments and is doing rather well

Patient's problem list includes but is not limited to bouts of hypercalcemia treated on the outside with normal saline after which the treatments have stopped, patient elected not to follow through with multiple myeloma chemotherapy his renal failure his creatinine of 2.46 that has risen to 3.38 currently patient does have diabetes well controlled with hemoglobin A1c of 4.8 coronary artery disease hypertension gastroesophageal reflux disease and obstructive uropathy of the prostate with a PSA of 6.2 currently

Labs: discussed as above

Social History: Patient is a writer having in fact published about himself in regards to fact and strong belief in the Almighty
                        FAITH

ALLERGIES: CHEESE, DEFINITY 2ML, OPTISON

Active Outpatient Medications (including Supplies):

Active Outpatient Medications	Status Refills	Issue Date Last Fill Expiration
1) DEXTRAN 70/HYPROMELLOSE 0.3% SOL 0.9ML	ACTIVE	Issu: 06-08-15

PATIENT NAME AND ADDRESS (Mechanical Imprinting, if available)
CALLIHAN, JOSEPH BEECHER
████████ FLORIDA ████

VISTA Electronic Medical Documentation
Printed at CW BILL YOUNG VAMC

Progress Notes

Printed On Aug 19, 2015

```
        Qty: 72 for 30 days   Sig: INSTILL 1      Refills: 3    Last:08-06-15
        DROP IN EACH EYE FOUR TIMES A DAY FOR                   Expr:06-08-16
        EYES
```

	Active Non-VA Medications	Refills	Start Date Expiration
1)	Non-VA FOLIC ACID 0.4MG TAB Sig: 0.8 MG MOUTH EVERY DAY	ACTIVE	
2)	Non-VA METOPROLOL (TARTRATE) 50MG TAB Sig: 50MG MOUTH TWICE A DAY	ACTIVE	
3)	Non-VA MULTIVITAMIN/MINERALS THERAPEUT CAP/TAB Sig: 1 TABLET MOUTH DAILY	ACTIVE	
4)	Non-VA NO NON-VA DRUGS, HERBALS OR OTC'S Sig: PER PATIENT INTERVIEW	ACTIVE	
5)	Non-VA POTASSIUM CHLORIDE 20MEQ SA TAB Sig: 20MEQ MOUTH EVERY DAY	ACTIVE	
6)	Non-VA RED YEAST RICE CAP/TAB Sig: MOUTH DAILY	ACTIVE	
7)	Non-VA SAW PALMETTO CAP/TAB Sig:	ACTIVE	

8 Total Medications

Past Medical History unchanged since last visit

Review of Systems:

Patient does not report any lethargy or weakness in association with hypercalcemia he is alert, oriented, and has not slowed down has no appetite changes no bowel or bladder habit changes all 10 systems considered Negative for other organ system issues today

Vital signs
BP:134/77 (08/17/2015 10:25)
Pain:0 (08/17/2015 10:25)
Pulse:52 (08/17/2015 10:25)
RR:18 (08/17/2015 10:25)
Temp:98.3 F [36.8 C] (08/17/2015 10:25)
Pulse ox: SVS - Vital Signs Selected   (max 1 occurrence or 30 days)
   No data available for PULSE OXIMETRY
99 (L/MIN)(%) (12/18/2014 12:34)
SVS - WEIGHT WITHIN 30 D   (max 1 occurrence or 30 days)
   Measurement DT   WEIGHT
                        LB(KG)[BMI]

08/17/2015 10:25   194(88.00)(29*)
BMI 28.7

VISTA Electronic Medical Documentation
Printed at CW BILL YOUNG VAMC

FLORIDA

JOSEPH CALLIHAN

Progress Notes

Printed On Aug 19, 2015

Weight last read Aug 17, 2015@10:25:14
Height last read Aug 17, 2015@10:25:14

Physical exam

Integument	tone turgor within normal limits WNL, no ecchymoses, old scars, Photodermatitis
HEENT	normocephalic, atraumatic, symmetrical, PERRLA, conjunctiva pink WNL
	TM WNL cerumen, nasopharynx, no significant erythema or congestion,
	No bruits of significance, R to L equal, no asymmetry noted
RESPe	BS+ right to left equal, no wheezing, no rubs, air entry with good expansion, no effusions, no sign of labored breathing at rest
COR	Heart NSR with no murmur, rub, gallop, heave, or lift no ectopy
ABD	Abdomen benign without masses or organomegaly no significant tendern
EXT	no clubbing or cyanosis, no malrotation, no edema, trace
CNS	no focality, R TO L equal and symmetrical, DTR symmetrical and equal
	No obvious deficits, no evidence of muscle wasting, cranial nerves WNL no noted tonicoclonic activity, no asterixis
Rectal	deferred.

Assessment: Dx acute exacerbation of renal failure with a possible association of multiple myeloma not on therapy as the patient defers due to his strong faith to obtain from interventions leaving his destiny in the faith of gout patient's other concerns include diabetes with a good hemoglobin A1c of 4.8 inconsistent with diabetics in addition he has hypertension gastroesophageal reflux and hypercalcemia which has been treated on the outside as well as at the VA with good results he does have obstructive uropathy with PSA of 6.2 on the rise but not symptomatic

Plan: Continued care with the VA on routine six-month followup appointment understanding that the patient has not allowed for interventions from nephrology clinic and further monitoring of his numbers both with the VA and through his health insurance optimum with Dr. fanA in his clinic on the outside to continue. AVOID GERD SIX FOOD GRPS

Patient to call or return if questions or concerns.

Healthy lifestyle encouraged including no smoking, minimal alcohol use, weight control and regular exercise as tolerated for age and condition. Maintain compliance with medications.

VISTA Electronic Medical Documentation
Printed at CW BILL YOUNG VAMC

FLORIDA

TESTIMONY OF A MIRACLE MAN

Progress Notes

Printed On Sep 21, 2016

```
09/09/2016 13:39   206(93.44)[30*]
BMI 30.5
Weight last read Sep 09, 2016@13:39:28
Height last read Sep 09, 2016@13:39:28

Physical exam

Integument    tone turgor within normal limits WNL, no ecchymoses, old scars,
              Photodermatitis
HEENT         normocephalic, atraumatic, symmetrical, PERRLA, conjunctiva pink WNL
              TM WNL cerumen, nasopharynx, no significant erythema or congestion,
              No bruits of significance, R to L equal, no asymmetry noted
RESP          BS+ right to left equal, no wheezing, no rubs, air entry with good
e             expansion, no effusions, no sign of labored breathing at rest
COR           Heart NSR with no murmur, rub, gallop, heave, or lift no ectopy
ABD           Abdomen benign without masses or organomegaly no significant tender

EXT           no clubbing or cyanosis, no malrotation, no edema, trace

CNS           no focality, R TO L equal and symmetrical, DTR symmetrical and equal
              No obvious deficits, no evidence of muscle wasting, cranial nerves
              WNL  no noted tonicoclonic activity,  no asterixis

Rectal        deferred.


Assessment: Dx renal failure multiple myeloma elevated PSA gastroesophageal
reflux and urinary infection symptoms with negative CNS. uti symptoms/rx self

RF stage III+

Plan:         Continuing patient's choice and method of treatment for urinary
tract infection now Alway are overriding seeing creatinine to 4.99 consistent
with low clearance and significant renal failure adjustment in intake of fluids
medications and natural substances with therefore limitations from inability to
eliminate or excrete them via the kidney had been clearly covered option to
follow through with kidney specialty nephrology as a consultation suggested
patient's decision pending

Return to clinic with regular appointment times and pre-appointment lab work for
close monitoring to continue


Patient to call or return if questions or concerns.

Healthy lifestyle encouraged including no smoking, minimal alcohol use,weight
control and regular exercise as tolerated for age and condition. Maintain
compliance with medications.

      Medication Reconciliation Review:
```

PATIENT NAME AND ADDRESS (Mechanical Imprinting, if available)
CALLIHAN, JOSEPH BEECHER
FLORIDA

VISTA Electronic Medical Documentation
Printed at C.W. BILL YOUNG DEPT OF VAMC

CHAPTER 6

A "Fun" Return Visit and satan Gets Involved

This chapter has some unbelievable information to report. First, let's get to the "fun" part. In May of 2016 (approximately two years after having turned down the chemo Dr. A. had offered), I visited once again, this time, to get copies of my medical records for use in writing this book. As I was waiting for the few pages to be printed, I observed Dr. A. go by and enter into his office. The door was open, and I watched as he sat down. He was not busy on the phone or otherwise, so I knocked on the entry and asked if I might come in and talk with him for a while.

Dr. A. said, "Sure, come on in." I entered and stood before his desk.

I said, "I don't know if you remember me or not, but I'm Joe Callihan, the guy who turned down your chemo treatment because of all the wonderful side effects it had."

Looking at me he responded by saying, "Yes, I remember you."

I must admit, I haven't a drop of effeminate blood in me. But I felt like a beauty queen, as I turned and swirled in front of him. He had told me if I did not do the chemo, I would become very weak, then delusional, and lastly dead.

"Do I look like I have no energy?" I asked. Then I said, "I'm really not delusional. I'm just Irish!" Lastly I said, "I think you will agree with me, I definitely am not dead!"

At this he said, "You know, God could still change His mind, and this could come back on you."

"Maybe the religious 'man upstairs' might. But My Heavenly Father loves me. He does not play such games. He has work for me to do." I thanked him for being so understanding, got my reports, and left.

Now let me tell you what I have been personally told by two of my doctors, first, Dr. Z. at the VA. Once when visiting him, he looked at me and said, "When I look at what your blood test says, everything about it screams at me saying, '*kidney failure*'! In fact, you should not be able to be standing before me right now. You should be in a hospital bed, weak, and in a lot of pain. But just look at you! You don't seem to lack energy nor do you look like you are in pain."

I said, "No, I'm not, Dr. Z."

Then he said to me, "There's only one way to explain it. That has to be God!"

It was so nice to know I have a doctor knows he is not God (as many with ego are inclined to believe).

On a recent visit with Dr. Fana to get the findings of my latest blood test, he, like Dr. Z., looked long at the computer screen which had the results of my blood test. Then looking at me he said, "I wish I had your faith. I'm not there yet, but I'm working on it." Then he followed by saying, "The results I see on this screen all say you have *kidney failure*. But looking at you standing in front of me, I can't find any of the symptoms. Do you realize you are violating the laws of medicine? There is only one explanation for this. It has to be God keeping you in His care."

It is so much fun, having God use me as an example of His perfect love, mercy, power, and grace. All honor and glory belong only to Him for this. I am only the vessel whose faith He has chosen to honor. I know one day, death will come knocking, not from satan, but from God. It will be my Father calling me to come home. All spiritual battles shall be over. I pray that before time comes, I will have given Him many solid reasons to be able to honestly tell me, "Welcome, my good and faithful servant, enter into your reward."

So far in my life, so little have I done to make that possible. I ask that God uses me as He did with St. Paul and that He turns my life around and makes me one of His success stories. I pray this prayer every day.

CHAPTER 7

The Good, Bad, and Ugly Lies

In the course of writing the account of how my Heavenly Father has answered my prayers and preserved my life, I thought perhaps it would be a good idea to present proof of what I have been testifying to. I know there are those of varying faith from little to none at all, who may be reading my book. What better proof can there be (other than looking at this live servant of God) than seeing the actual reports from the doctors involved.

Therefore, the following pages contain copies of the actual medical reports from my doctors. In them, you will find the good news, by which God has chosen to keep me alive, namely, my unwavering faith in His perfect love for me, His servant, and redeemed son. You also will see all of the many medical issues which have been trying to destroy my body and end my life. These are true reports from the time I was first told I had cancer.

But only recently did I request the reports from Dr. Fana's records. I needed them to help me complete this book, for the benefit of unbelievers. You cannot imagine how shocked and angry I became at finding reports of me having been an alcoholic for over twenty years of my life. Also, in giving my life over to Jesus Christ, He delivered me from this evil. As good as that may sound, I know Jesus has done this in the lives of all who sincerely come to Him for deliverance. In my case, it is nothing but lies!

I went to visit Dr. Fana and presented to him these false reports on my record, demanding they be removed. He was of like mind, even like me, having become angry at what was written. He did some fast research and discovered the source may well have been the proctologist who was advising Dr. B., based on the information obtained from my blood test. The test showed me to have cirrhosis of the liver (as you will note on page 63 of the report).

From this finding, someone (perhaps the proctologist) dreamed up a fantastic imaginary story about me having been an alcoholic. Not one word of which was or is true! Dr. Fana told me I do have this disease, but it is from fatty tissue on my liver, not from alcoholic consumption. Dr. Fana has promised to get to the source of this and report his finding to me. He also has assured me it will be thoroughly made correct in my medical report, for all of which I am grateful. The only reason I decided to show the false report in this book is to give me opportunity to tell my story concerning alcohol. But can you imagine, had I not gotten a copy of this report with its abundance of lies about me, before I was called home?

I am a Christian writer. I write spiritual books under the influence of the Holy Spirit. Many of my books cry out to those enslaved in "religion," urging them to turn from religion, and the false bride, which teaches and supports it. Turn to the loving relationship which Jesus came to restore between us and our Heavenly Father. Ask for the Holy Spirit to lead and guide you to attending a church which is a member of the true body and bride of Christ.

You can learn more in my book, *Fill Me with the Fire of Your Love*. I used the pen name of Carlote Bengemyre to confound the "religious" who will be very angry with me over the contents of that book.

TESTIMONY OF A MIRACLE MAN

Copies from My Medical Records

LAB: CBC (INCLUDES DIFF/PLT) (Ordered for 05/27/2015)
LAB: HEMOGLOBIN A1c (Ordered for 05/27/2015)
LAB: VITAMIN B12/FOLATE, SERUM PANEL (Ordered for 05/27/2015)
LAB: FERRITIN (Ordered for 05/27/2015)
LAB: TSH W/REFLEX TO FT4 (Ordered for 05/27/2015)
LAB: PTH, INTACT (WITHOUT CALCIUM) (Ordered for 05/27/2015)
LAB: FECAL GLOBIN BY IMMUNOCHEMISTRY (Ordered for 05/27/2015)
Notes: due to the hypercalcemia
monitor the calcium together with the phosphorus and iPTH
will get a PTHr peptide.

10. Cachexia (M)
Continue Vitamin B12 Tablet, 100 MCG, 1 tablet, Orally, Once a day ; Continue Folic Acid Tablet, 800 MCG, 1 tablet, Orally, Once a day ; Continue Ferrous Sulfate Tablet, 325 (65 Fe) MG, 1 tablet, Orally, Once a day .
Notes: we discussed high calory meals like peanut butter and chocolate shakes with whey, protein shakes with branched chain amino acids (BCAA).

11. Unspecified thrombocytopenia (M)
Notes: do not use a blade when shaving
draw blood with a butterfly.

12. Alcoholic cirrhosis of liver (M)
Notes: he has been off the bottle many years
we suggested milk thistle.

13. Other and unspecified alcohol dependence, in remission (M)
Notes: cont strong support circle at church.

14. Diabetes with neurological manifestations, type II or unspecified type, not stated as uncontrolled (M)
Notes: alpha lipoic acid.

15. Polyneuropathy in diabetes (M)
Notes: visit with podiatry.

16. Sciatica
Notes: I told Joe I think his pain is due to the mets on the left femoral shaft and we should probably get an xray
to make sure its not worsening
since the pain is not severe, he has deferred, but if it increases in intensity, I will push him more
heat and massage
avoid sleeping on that side
increase dose of tumeric.

Therapeutic Injections:
Cyanocobalamin : 1 mg (Dose No:1) given by ▓▓▓▓ on left deltoid

Labs:
Lab: PTH-Related Peptide (PTH-rP)
Procedure Codes: J3420 INJ VIT B-12 CYNOCOBLMN TO 1000 MCG
Follow Up: 10 Weeks for labs and follow after

Provider: ▓▓▓▓ MD
Patient: Callihan, Joseph B DOB: ▓▓▓▓ Date: 01/27/2015

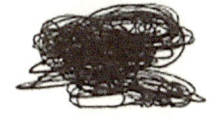

9/30/2016

JOSEPH CALLIHAN

performed: sensations diminished, Pedal pulse taking performed: 1+.

Assessment:
Assessment:
1. Body Mass Index 25.0-25.9, adult - V85.21 (Primary)
2. Multiple myeloma, without mention of having achieved remission (M) - 203.00
3. Diabetes with renal manifestations, type II or unspecified type, not stated as uncontrolled (M) - 250.40
4. Chronic kidney disease, Stage IV (severe) - 585.4
5. Secondary malignant neoplasm of bone and bone marrow (M) - 198.5
6. Secondary malignant neoplasm of other digestive organs and spleen - 197.8
7. Chronic Angina Pectoris (M) - 413.9
8. Chronic airway obstruction, not elsewhere classified (M) - 496
9. Hypoparathyroidism (M) - 252.1, see labs done 3/20/2014
10. Cachexia (M) - 799.4
11. Unspecified thrombocytopenia (M) - 287.5
12. Alcoholic cirrhosis of liver (M) - 571.2
13. Other and unspecified alcohol dependence, in remission (M) - 303.93
14. Diabetes with neurological manifestations, type II or unspecified type, not stated as uncontrolled (M) - 250.60
15. Polyneuropathy in diabetes (M) - 357.2
16. Sciatica - 724.3

Plan:
1. Body Mass Index 25.0-25.9, adult
Notes: I encouraged him to eat high calory foods since he will lose weight as the disease progresses.

2. Multiple myeloma, without mention of having achieved remission (M)
Notes: I spoke to Joe Christian to Christian and I think he should have repeat imaging and see if the disease is getting worse and better. I truly am impressed how he does not have any bone pain with the lesions on the bone. He will consider it.

3. Diabetes with renal manifestations, type II or unspecified type, not stated as uncontrolled (M)
Continue Amlodipine Besylate Tablet, 10 MG, 1 tablet, Orally, Once a day.

4. Chronic kidney disease, Stage IV (severe)
Continue Ferrous Sulfate Tablet, 325 (65 Fe) MG, 1 tablet, Orally, Once a day ; Continue Amlodipine Besylate Tablet, 10 MG, 1 tablet, Orally, Once a day.
Notes: recheck the microalb / cvreat ratio in 10 weeks when he returns and add hydralazine or isosorbide if his BP tolerates.

5. Secondary malignant neoplasm of bone and bone marrow (M)
Notes: we will discuss rechecking the imaging but this time with a CT of the Abd and Pelvis as suggested by Dr Mangat.

6. Secondary malignant neoplasm of other digestive organs and spleen
Notes: as above
cont to talk to the patient about rechecking the imaging.

7. Chronic Angina Pectoris (M)
Continue Metoprolol Tartrate Tablet, 50 MG, 1 tablet, Orally, Twice a day.

8. Chronic airway obstruction, not elsewhere classified (M)
Notes: refuses vaccine since he claims he does not believe in htem
please see refusal of treatment form.

9. Hypoparathyroidism (M)
Continue Alendronate Sodium Tablet, 10 MG, 1 tablet, Orally, Once a day.
LAB: MICROALBUMIN, RANDOM URINE (W/CREATININE) (Ordered for 05/27/2015)
LAB: LIPID PANEL (Ordered for 05/27/2015)
LAB: COMPREHENSIVE METABOLIC PANEL (Ordered for 05/27/2015)
LAB: PHOSPHATE (AS PHOSPHORUS) (Ordered for 05/27/2015)

9/30/2016

TESTIMONY OF A MIRACLE MAN

Tablet 1 tablet Once a day, Unknown Ferrous Sulfate 325 (65 Fe) MG Tablet 1 tablet Once a day, Unknown Alendronate Sodium 10 MG Tablet 1 tablet Once a day, Unknown Potassium Chloride Crys ER 20 MEQ Tablet Extended Release 1 tablet once a day, Unknown Amlodipine Besylate 10 MG Tablet 1 tablet Once a day, Unknown Metoprolol Tartrate 50 MG Tablet 1 tablet Twice a day, Unknown Red Yeast Rice 600 MG Capsule 1 capsule once a day, Notes: (Mig), Unknown Slo-Niacin 500 MG Tablet Extended Release 1 tablet Once a day, Notes: (Mig), Unknown Flomax 0.4 MG Capsule 1 capsule 30 minutes after the same meal each day Once a day, Unknown Magnesium Oxide 420 MG Tablet 1 tablet Once a day, Unknown CINNAMON PLUS CHROMIUM 1000 MG 1 capsule once a day, Notes: (Mig), Unknown Ammonium Lactate 12 % Cream 1 application to affected area Twice a day, Notes: (Mig), Unknown Turmeric 450 MG Capsule 1 capsule once a day, Notes: (Mig), Unknown Cascara Sagrada 450 MG Capsule 1 capsule Twice a day, Notes: (Mig), Unknown Ubiquinol 100 MG Capsule, Unknown Cranberry 250 MG Capsule, Medication List reviewed and reconciled with the patient

Allergies: Yogurt: (Mig) 1/18/2014 GI Upset: Allergy, Cheese: (Mig) 1/18/2014 GI Upset: Allergy, Definity: (Mig) 1/18/2014 Groin Pain: Allergy, Optison: (Mig) 1/18/2014 Unknown: Allergy.

Objective:
Vitals: Temp 97.4 F, BP 120/62 mm Hg, HR 56 /min, RR 14 /min, Oxygen sat % 99 %, Ht 70 in, Wt 177 lbs, BMI 25.39 Index, Wt-kg 80.29.

Past Orders:
Lab:PTH, INTACT AND CALCIUM

Collection Date	01/15/2015	11/21/2014	10/02/2014
Order Date	01/15/2015	11/21/2014	10/02/2014
CALCIUM	10.5 H (8.6-10.3 mg/dL)	13.1 H (8.6-10.3 mg/dL)	TNP (mg/dL)
PARATHYROID HORMONE,SINTACT	5 L (14-64 pg/mL)	7 L (14-64 pg/mL)	TNP (pg/mL)
Clinical Info:		Please fax results to 727-384-0192 Please fax results to 727-384-0192	

Lab:TSH, 3RD GENERATION

Collection Date	01/15/2015	08/22/2014	02/14/2014
Order Date	01/15/2015	08/22/2014	02/14/2014
TSH	4.47 (0.40-4.50 mIU/L)	2.38 (0.40-4.50 mIU/L)	2.95 (0.40-4.50 mIU/L)

Lab:LIPID PANEL

Collection Date	01/15/2015	08/22/2014	05/07/2014
Order Date	01/15/2015	08/22/2014	05/07/2014
TRIGLYCERIDES	88 (<150 mg/dL)	153 H (<150 mg/dL)	107 (<150 mg/dL)
CHOLESTEROL, TOTAL	100 L (125-200 mg/dL)	107 L (125-200 mg/dL)	135 (125-200 mg/dL)
HDL CHOLESTEROL	29 L (> OR = 40 mg/dL)	22 L (> OR = 40 mg/dL)	30 L (> OR = 40 mg/dL)
LDL-CHOLESTEROL	53 (<130 mg/dL (calc))	54 (<130 mg/dL (calc))	84 (<130 mg/dL (calc))
CHOL/HDLC RATIO	3.4 (< OR = 5.0 (calc))	4.9 (< OR = 5.0 (calc))	4.5 (< OR = 5.0 (calc))
NON HDL CHOLESTEROL	71 (mg/dL (calc))	85 (mg/dL (calc))	105 (mg/dL (calc))

Lab:CBC (INCLUDES DIFF/PLT)

9/30/2016

JOSEPH CALLIHAN

Progress Notes

Patient: Callihan, Joseph B
Account Number: ▮
DOB: ▮ Age: 70 Y Sex: Male
Phone: ▮
Address: ▮ FL ▮

Provider: ▮ MD
Date: 01/27/2015

Subjective:
Chief Complaints:
1. Pt presents today for 3 month follow up with lab review. 2. Pt complains that at times he get pain in Left side hip joint pain that shoots down his leg and feet pain. 3. He is also here for the follow up of his hypercalcemia, Diabetes and COPD. 4. He refuses to undergo treatment for the Myeloma.

HPI:
General:
He says he is feeling better. He has little fatigue and his appetite has improved some what. He still adamant about not getting treatment and he has faith Jesus Christ will take care of him. He does not drink alcohol anymore and has given himself to our Saviour. He is ready to accept death if it were the wish of God and he prays often about this. Being a Christian, I have to admit with the disease burden he has from the Myeloma with mets to the bones and the spleen as well as the anemia, his Diabetes and a cirrhotic liver from years of drinking, it i a miracle that he is still alive.

He has sharp pains going from his buttock to the ankle but he also has pain on his feet which he does not want medicines for and he is able to sleep OK. Pains are well controlled with turmeric, ubiquinone the alendronate has helped the bone pain.

ROS:
GENERAL:
Constitutional Weight gain, Weight loss, Fatigue, Appetite decreased. Cardiovascular Negative. Respiratory Negative. Gastrointestinal Heart burn. Neurological pain on the hip rdiating to the ankle 3/10 and pain on the feet 2/10.

Medical History: Non-Secretory Myeloma (Oncology 5/2014), Secondary Malignant Lesions of Bone (lytic lesions on the R frontal clavarium and left prox femoral shaftsecondary to Multiple Myeloma on Skeletal Survey Bone Scan 4/2014), Secondary Malignant Lesions of Spleen (secondary to Multiple Myeloma;Abdominal US 10/2/2014), DM Type II with renal manifestations, Hypertension, Aortic Sclerosis without stenosis (ECHO 2/2014), Aortic Insufficiency (ECHO 2/2014), Mitral Valve Insufficiency (ECHO 2/2014), Hyperlipidemia, Previous Myocardial Infarct (2006), S/P Coronary Artery Bypass Grafting x 3 vessels (2006), Atherosclerosis of Native Coronary Artery , Chronic Stable Angina, COPD (mild; Spirometry 2/2014), Chronic Constipation, Cirrhosis of the Liver (Abdominal U/S 4/2014), Elevated Alkaline Phosphatase (Labs 10/2014; 7/2014; 2/2014), Splenomegaly (Abdominal U/S 4/2014), Thrombocytopenia (Platelets 124,000 1/15/2015, Chronic Kidney Disease Stage IV (GFR = 23 on 11/2014 and 26 on 1/15/2015), Cachexia with BMI between 24-25 and Albumin between 3.6 to 3.4 from 2014-2015 (See Oncology notes), BPH with obstruction , Anemia secondary to neoplastic disease and chronic kidney disease (Labs 1/15/2015 11/2014; 10/2014), Vitamin B12 Deficiency (Labs 5/2014), Folate Deficiency (Labs 2/2014), Vitamin D Deficiency (Labs 2/2014), Hypoparathyroidism (Labs 11/2014; 3/2014), Hypercalcemia (Labs 11/2014; 10/2014; 7/2014), Hypokalemia (Labs 10/2014; 2/2014), Weight Loss and Tumor Cachexia, Hyper Gammaglobulinemia A due to Myeloma secretion, Alcohol Dependence in remission (See Social History taken 1/15/2015).

Surgical History: Coronary Artery Bypass Grafting x 3 vessels (unknown) 2006, Laparoscopic Cholecystectomy 2007.

Social History:
Drugs/Alcohol: Substance Dependence: In remission from alcohol dependence for more than 20 years He has been to AA He drank despite having many health issues Tried to quit many times and was not able to until he found Jesus Christ Alcohol was taken in larger amount and for longer period than intended Tolerance (needed more to produce the buzz-effect) which led to ingesting great quantities .

Medications: Unknown Vitamin B12 100 MCG Tablet 1 tablet Once a day, Unknown Folic Acid 800 MCG

9/30/2016

TESTIMONY OF A MIRACLE MAN

Callihan, Joseph B
71 Y old Male, DOB:
Account Number:
FL
Home:
Guarantor: Callihan, Joseph B   Insurance:
ID: 20133
Ph: Referring: Dr
Appointment Facility:

12/08/2015   Progress Notes: ARNP

Current Medications

Taking
- Omeprazole 40 MG Capsule Delayed Release 1 capsule Once a day
- Amlodipine Besylate 10 MG Tablet 1 tablet Once a day
- Potassium Chloride Crys ER 20 MEQ Tablet Extended Release 1 tablet once a day
- Flomax 0.4 MG Capsule 1 capsule 30 minutes after the same meal each day Once a day
- Magnesium Oxide 420 MG Tablet 1 tablet Once a day
- Turmeric 450 MG Capsule 1 capsule once a day, Notes: (Mlg)
- Cascara Sagrada 450 MG Capsule 1 capsule Twice a day prn constipation, Notes: (Mlg)
- Folic Acid 800 MCG Tablet 1 tablet Once a day
- Ferrous Sulfate 325 (65 Fe) MG Tablet 1 tablet every now and then
- Alendronate Sodium 70 MG Tablet 1 tablet Once a day
- Vitamin B12 100 MCG Tablet 1 tablet Once a day
- CINNAMON PLUS CHROMIUM 1000 MG 1 capsule once a day, Notes: (Mlg)
- Ubiquinol 100 MG Capsule
- Slo-Niacin 500 MG Tablet Extended Release 1 tablet Once a day, Notes: (Mlg)
- Cranberry 250 MG Capsule
- Metoprolol Tartrate 50 MG Tablet 1 tablet Twice a day

Discontinued
- Ammonium Lactate 12 % Cream 1 application to affected area Twice a day, Notes: (Mlg)
- Medication List reviewed and reconciled with the patient

Past Medical History

Non-Secretory Myeloma (Oncology 5/2014)
Secondary Malignant Lesions of Bone (lytic lesions on the R frontal cranium and left prox femoral shaft secondary to Multiple Myeloma on Skeletal Survey Bone Scan 4/2014)
Secondary Malignant Lesions of

Reason for Appointment

1. Patient present today for 3 months follow up with labs and for his chronic conditions

History of Present Illness

General:
Presents today for 3 month f/u with lab review.
States that he has been feeling wonderful and he has no concerns today. He states that God is taking care of his chronic medical conditions. Whatever God has in store for his health and future he is ok with.

Vital Signs

BP 114/60 mm Hg, HR 77 /min, RR 14 /min, Oxygen sat % 95 %, Ht 70 in, Wt 207 lbs, BMI 29.70 Index, Wt-kg 93.89.

Past Orders

Lab:URINE DRUG SCREEN 1 (Order Date - 11/24/2015) (Collection Date - 11/24/2015)

MARIJUANA	negative	-
COMMENT	SEE NOTE	-
AMPHETAMINES	negative	-
BARBITURATES	negative	-
BENZODIAZEPINES	negative	-
COCAINE	negative	-
METHADONE	negative	-
OPIATES	negative	-
PCP (PHENCYCLIDINE)	negative	-
PROPOXYPHENE	negative	-
ETHANOL	negative	-

Lab:HEMOGLOBIN A1c

Collection Date	11/24/2015	07/28/2015	04/02/2015
Order Date	11/24/2015	07/28/2015	04/02/2015
HEMOGLOBIN A1c	5.2 (<5.7 % of total Hgb)	5.0 (<5.7 % of total Hgb)	5.0 (<5.7 % of total Hgb)

Lab:VITAMIN B12/FOLATE, SERUM PANEL

Collection Date	11/24/2015	07/28/2015	04/02/2015
Order Date	11/24/2015	07/28/2015	04/02/2015
FOLATE, SERUM	>24.0 (ng/mL)	9.5 (ng/mL)	6.6 (ng/mL)
VITAMIN B12	480	845	654

Patient: Callihan, Joseph B   DOB: Progress Note: , ARNP   12/08/2015
Note generated by

9/30/2016

JOSEPH CALLIHAN

Callihan, Joseph B
71 Y old Male, DOB: 03/20/1944

03/17/2016

Progress Notes: ARNP

Current Medications

Taking
- Omeprazole 40 MG Capsule Delayed Release 1 capsule Once a day
- Amlodipine Besylate 10 MG Tablet 1 tablet Once a day
- Potassium Chloride Crys ER 20 MEQ Tablet Extended Release 1 tablet once a day
- Magnesium Oxide 400 MG Tablet 1 tablet Once a day
- Turmeric 450 MG Capsule 1 capsule once a day, Notes: (Mlg)
- Cascara Sagrada 450 MG Capsule 1 capsule Twice a day prn constipation, Notes: (Mlg)
- Folic Acid 800 MCG Tablet 1 tablet Once a day
- Ferrous Sulfate 325 (65 Fe) MG Tablet 1 tablet every now and then
- Vitamin B12 100 MCG Tablet 1 tablet Once a day
- CINNAMON PLUS CHROMIUM 1000 MG 1 capsule once a day, Notes: (Mlg)
- Ubiquinol 100 MG Capsule
- Slo-Niacin 500 MG Tablet Extended Release 1 tablet Once a day, Notes: (Mlg)
- Cranberry 250 MG Capsule
- Metoprolol Tartrate 50 MG Tablet 1 tablet Twice a day
- Flomax 0.4 MG Capsule 1 capsule 30 minutes after the same meal each day Once a day
- Alendronate Sodium 10 MG Tablet 1 tablet Once a week
- Medication list reviewed and reconciled with the patient

Past Medical History

Non-Secretory Myeloma (Oncology 5/2014)
Secondary Malignant Lesions of Bone (lytic lesions on the R frontal clavarium and left prox femoral shafts secondary to Multiple Myeloma on Skeletal Survey Bone Scan 4/2014)
Secondary Malignant Lesions of Spleen (secondary to Multiple Myeloma Abdominal US 10/2/2014)
Hypertension
Aortic Sclerosis without stenosis

Reason for Appointment
1. Pt presents today for 3 months follow up

History of Present Illness

General:
Presents today for 3 month f/u with lab review. Renal function is steady. He is anti Referrals and anti-meds due to side effects of Meds. Mainly prefers Vitamins. No acute complaints.
He says that God is his healer. He refuses ever getting Flu shot again as it gave him a large itchy skin reaction over the Holidays.
He is a self-proclaimed "walking miracle". He stays busy writing his Christian medical stories. He feels great, has no fears be of God's constant presence.
Presents today for 3 month f/u with lab review.
States that he has been feeling wonderful and he has no concerns today. He states that God is taking care of his chronic medical conditions. Whatever God has in store for his health and future he is ok with.

Vital Signs
BP 120/70 mm Hg, HR 75 /min, RR 14 /min, Oxygen sat % 98 %, Ht 70 in, Wt 210 lbs, BMI 30.13 Index, Wt-kg 95.26.

Past Orders

Lab: PSA, TOTAL

Collection Date	03/07/2016	01/11/2016	01/15/2015
Order Date	03/07/2016	01/11/2016	01/15/2015
PSA, TOTAL	4.9 H (< OR = 4.0 ng/mL)	4.8 H (< OR = 4.0 ng/mL)	4.6 H (< OR = 4.0 ng/mL)

Lab: VITAMIN B12/FOLATE, SERUM PANEL

Collection Date	03/07/2016	01/11/2016	11/24/2015
Order Date	03/07/2016	01/11/2016	11/24/2015
FOLATE, SERUM	7.0 (ng/mL)	11.6 (ng/mL)	>24.0 (ng/mL)
VITAMIN B12	478 (200-1100 pg/mL)	618 (200-1100 pg/mL)	480 (200-1100 pg/mL)

Lab: HEMOGLOBIN A1c

Collection Date	03/07/2016	01/11/2016	11/24/2015
Order Date	03/07/2016	01/11/2016	11/24/2015
HEMOGLOBIN A1c	5.1 (<5.7 % of total Hgb)	5.4 (<5.7 % of total Hgb)	5.2 (<5.7 % of total Hgb)

TESTIMONY OF A MIRACLE MAN

Page 3 of 70

Callihan, Joseph B
72 Y old Male, DOB: ▉▉▉▉
Account Number: ▉▉▉▉
Home: ▉▉▉▉, FL
Guarantor: Callihan, Joseph B   Insurance: ▉▉▉▉
                                 ID: ▉▉▉▉
PCP: ▉▉▉▉, M.D.   Referring: ▉▉▉▉, M.D.
Appointment Facility: ▉▉▉▉ Medical Group

06/29/2016   Progress Notes: ▉▉▉▉, ARNP

Current Medications

Taking
- Metoprolol Tartrate 50 MG Tablet 1 tablet Twice a day
- Flomax 0.4 MG Capsule 1 capsule 30 minutes after the same meal each day Once a day
- Tums 500 MG Tablet Chewable 1 tablet Four times a day

Not-Taking/PRN
- Omeprazole 40 MG Capsule Delayed Release 1 capsule Once a day
- Amlodipine Besylate 10 MG Tablet 1 tablet Once a day
- Potassium Chloride Crys ER 20 MEQ Tablet Extended Release 1 tablet once a day
- Magnesium Oxide 420 MG Tablet 1 tablet Once a day
- Turmeric 450 MG Capsule 1 capsule once a day, Notes: (Mig)
- Cascara Sagrada 450 MG Capsule 1 capsule Twice a day prn constipation, Notes: (Mig)
- Folic Acid 800 MCG Tablet 1 tablet Once a day
- Ferrous Sulfate 325 (65 Fe) MG Tablet 1 tablet every now and then
- Vitamin B12 100 MCG Tablet 1 tablet Once a day
- CINNAMON PLUS CHROMIUM 1000 MG 1 capsule once a day, Notes: (Mig)
- Ubiquinol 100 MG Capsule
- Slo-Niacin 500 MG Tablet Extended Release 1 tablet Once a day, Notes: (Mig)
- Cranberry 250 MG Capsule
- Alendronate Sodium 10 MG Tablet 1 tablet Once a week

Past Medical History

Non-Secretory Myeloma (Oncology 5/2014)
Secondary Malignant Lesions of Bone (lytic lesions on the R frontal clavarium and left prox femoral shaft secondary to Multiple Myeloma on Skeletal Survey Bone Scan 4/2014)
Secondary Malignant Lesions of Spleen (secondary to Multiple Myeloma; Abdominal US 10/2/2014)
Hypertension

Reason for Appointment

1. Pt presents today for 3 month follow up of his chronic conditions and also for lab review

History of Present Illness

General:
Presents today for 3 month f/u with lab review.
He has been feeling great. He is really not taking any medications but the one for his blood pressure and his prostate. He is not taking anything else b/c he really doesn't see the need for them. He has placed his trust in God to cure him of all his ailments.
His only complaint is he his having bilat shoulder pain. Doesn't want anything for it b/c it is just an ache but that is his only issue.

Vital Signs

BP 120/80 mm Hg, HR 96 /min, RR 14 /min, Oxygen sat % 98 %, Ht 70 in, Wt 210 lbs, BMI 30.13 Index, Wt-kg 95.26.

Past Orders

Lab:HEMOGLOBIN A1c

Collection Date	06/17/2016	03/07/2016	01/11/2016
Order Date	06/17/2016	03/07/2016	01/11/2016
HEMOGLOBIN A1c	5.2 (<5.7 % of total Hgb)	5.1 (<5.7 % of total Hgb)	5.4 (<5.7 % of total Hgb)

Lab:PTH, INTACT (WITHOUT CALCIUM)

Collection Date	06/17/2016	11/24/2015	07/28/2015
Order Date	06/17/2016	11/24/2015	07/28/2015
PARATHYROID HORMONE,	20 (14-64 pg/mL)	6 L (14-64 pg/mL)	6 L (14-64 pg/mL)

Lab:PSA (FREE AND TOTAL)

Collection Date	06/17/2016	11/24/2015	07/28/2015
Order Date	06/17/2016	11/24/2015	07/28/2015
FREE PSA	2.3 (ng/mL)	3.6 (ng/mL)	3.5 (ng/mL)
TOTAL PSA	6.1 H (< OR = 4.0 ng/mL)	8.4 H (< OR = 4.0 ng/mL)	6.4 H (< OR = 4.0 ng/mL)
% FREE PSA	38 (>25 % (calc))	43 (>25 % (calc))	55 (>25 % (calc))

Lab:VITAMIN B12/FOLATE, SERUM PANEL.

Patient: Callihan, Joseph B   DOB: ▉▉▉▉   Progress Note: ▉▉▉▉, ARNP   06/29/2016

9/30/2016

CHAPTER 8

Alcohol and Me: The True Story

Thanks be to God, I never have been interested in alcohol nor in becoming an alcoholic. You see, my mother was an alcoholic for most of her life. It was not until the late years of her life, she surrendered to Jesus, asking Him to deliver her from alcohol. He did! But, as a child, sometimes one of my friends would invite me to spend a sleepover at their home. Receiving permission, I would. However, there would come the time when my friend would ask the normal question, "How come you never invite me to a sleepover at your house?" Then I would have to try coming up with a new excuse, different from the one I had given when asked this same question before.

 I could never bring myself to tell of the embarrassment I might experience if I did. My mother was living with my grandparents, who raised me and my sister. I never knew who would be coming home from work, a normal, intelligent person or a stupid drunk.

The source for my mother's having turned to alcohol is revealed in my book, *Love Poems for Dodie*, which I dedicated to my late, wonderful, and most beautiful wife, Dolores Nichols-Callihan. I lost her to cancer in October 2011. We shared fifty-one months of wedded bliss together. I loved her with all of my heart.

But I digress. This is to be about me and alcohol. Basically, I hate the stuff and always have. Seeing the damages it did to my mother's life and has done in the lives of so many, I find no use for it in my life. I served in the Navy and, on several occasions, was invited to go out drinking with my shipmates. I was no prude, so I went. In my book, *Adventures in Navyland*, you can read of my experience on a visit to a strip club in Charleston, SC with two of my buddies. I dare you to read of my encounter with the headliner and try not to break up laughing ("Was it something I said?").

Would you believe I once quit my job because of pressure to go out drinking with some of the upper echelon, in order to be promoted? OK, I may as well tell you the whole story. Especially as it glorifies God. I will call it Jim's story. Jim is now departed, but I believe he would not mind my sharing his story with you here and now.

In my late twenties, I began what was to be my first attempt in the retail business. I found myself working for Sears, Roebuck & Company in the building materials department. Although I knew almost nothing about the materials involved (having never worked in the building industry), nevertheless, I was a quick study. One thing I became known for was I absolutely refused to lie, in order to make a sale. If I did not know the answer, I would find a source to give me the answer, either a book or a fellow salesman. I was succeeding fairly well in selling. In fact, people would send their friends to buy from me, because I had insisted on being honest with them.

One day, I was called to go see Mr. Fisher, head of the personnel department. He was the man who had made the choice to give me the job. Arriving, Mr. Fisher told me there was an opening coming up for department manager trainee. He said the quality of work I had been doing in the building materials department had been noticed. He wanted to ask if I would be interested in being a contender.

I said "Yes, I greatly appreciate having been considered a candidate."

Mr. Fisher said, "I cannot guarantee it will be you. At present, it's between you and two others. But soon we will be making our decision."

Two days later, Jim, the manager of the sporting goods department, came to see me while I was working in the building dept. He introduced himself to me and told me I was the candidate selected to be the manager trainee. "Congratulations!" We shook hands as he informed me, "Starting tomorrow you will begin working with me in the sporting goods department."

This began my effort to advance to department manager. I took every management course they had to offer, scoring As and Bs on each one. When I was bought an invoice sheet, to sign my acceptance of merchandise into the department, I knew what every code on it meant.

I had known the lady over the receiving department from high school. I had her teach me the meaning of every code having to do with receiving. Likewise, I had a lady working in the accounting department, teaching me the meaning of every accounting code on the invoice sheet.

On occasion, when brought the invoice to sign, I would notice either a receiving or accounting code which was a mistake. I would refuse to sign and immediately took the invoice to the necessary department and get the mistake corrected. The person whom I verified the mistake with and then asked to make the corrections would say to me, "That's an accounting code, how did you catch it?"

I would reply, "I made it my business to know what the code means."

Meanwhile, I had quickly gotten to where Jim, at lunch time, would leave the department in my care, announcing he would be back later. Later was the correct word. We would not see Jim again, until it was time to hit the time clock and go home. Where had he been for all of that time? He had been in the cafeteria, talking with and laughing with his upper echelon buddies.

I had been working for Sears for a year and seven months and had more than proven my management abilities several times over. So one day, I asked Jim to go to the cafeteria with me, saying I would buy his coffee. I told him I had something I wanted to talk with him about. Once there and seated at a table, I began my questioning.

"Jim, I've been manager trainee for quite some time now. I've taken every management course available and made As and Bs on every one of them. You know the kind of job I have been doing while you turned the department over to me. There is not a single department in this store I could not effectively manage. I would like to know what it is that is holding up me being promoted?"

Here, I suppose I should make note about Jim. He was married, having a beautiful wife and two daughters. However, he had a bad flaw. He would go out with anything wearing a dress. It was well known all over the store, the many female employees he had fooled around with. A little trouble being faithful to the vows of marriage he had once made.

In answering my question, Jim began by telling me, "Joe, getting ahead has more to do than just the quality of work you turn in. It also has to do with knowing and associating with the 'right people.'"

When I said, "I'm not sure what you are telling me?"

Jim then stated the facts of the matter. "Some of the staff members often will go out and hit the bars after work, myself included. Many times you have been invited to join us. But you've always had some excuse not to go. One of the guys would ask, 'Where's Callihan?' Another would answer, 'Oh, he had an excuse not to join us tonight.' The one who had asked would shout, 'Again!'"

At this, I told him my reason. "Jim, I don't drink alcoholic beverages. I happen to like Coca-Cola. I have found that usually there is some moron, who, when the more they have to drink, object to my drinking Coke. Once, at a party I was attending, I even caught a guy trying to pour something he had in a flask into my coke. I grabbed his wrist and turned him away. He got angry because it caused him to spill some of his drink. Then he said he would be more careful not to get caught the next time he tried. At this, I warned him on any next time, I would literally beat the hell out of him. I will kid around about it for a while. But if it gets more serious, I'm more than willing to beat the hell out of the agitator. I don't believe my chance for promotion would improve, if I had to take one of the staff members outside and beat the hell out of him. So I try to avoid such a thing happening. That's why I don't hang out in bars."

In his answer, Jim said, "You know, in some parts of the world, they get insulted if you don't burp after eating the meal they made. In other places, a man gets insulted if you don't sleep with his wife."

To this, I replied, "But maybe I'd be insulted. I don't live my life to please other people. First, I try to please God, then myself. Other people come last. If you don't understand that, I feel sorry for you."

At this, we parted. I knew I needed to take another approach. I was determined I would go speak with the new personnel manager the next day. He was recently hired to replace Mr. Fisher, who had chosen to join the FBI. As it turns out, he was fresh out of college, a first-class snob, and the only reason he was here was because his father managed a large Sears store in Mississippi. What I was unaware of was he and Jim were drinking buddies.

So I went to the personnel manager to see what could be done to help me advance. I began by stating the kind of effort I had been putting out, which I believed showed I was well qualified. I said I did not believe Jim was giving me an accurate appraisal of my abilities. I requested to be transferred to another department and to work under a different manager for six weeks, then get an evaluation from him. If he does not say I put out 110 percent effort, then fire me.

I was serious in my challenge. But to my surprise the jerk said to me, "We can't do that, as there's no opening in any department." I knew at once that was a lie. There were three openings, which every employee was aware of. Then the PM said, "Perhaps you'd be happier somewhere else? Why don't you think about it and give me your decision later?" *Talk about a hint!*

I was up till after midnight, hand peck typing out my letter of resignation. The next morning, I was in the personnel office. "Mr. Jerk (can't remember this little nothing's name), I want to thank you for not just firing me after our conversation yesterday." He went to say something, but I interrupted. "Even though I've never heard about someone being fired for doing an excellent job, nevertheless, you did give me an option, and I would like to exercise that option, by handing you my letter of resignation, effective immediately."

He took the letter from my hand saying, "If that is what you wish."

I must admit, his casual remark made my Irish temper flare a bit. "I've wasted a year and seven months of my life, working for a company that expects you to be a stupid drunk in order to get promoted. No More!" I then turned and left.

A little later in the day, Jim came up to me. "I understand you turned in your letter of resignation."

"Yes," was my reply.

"Have you found something else yet?"

I said "No, but I'm not worried. Whoever gets me will have a top-notch employee."

At this, Jim responded with, "Well, Joe, someday you'll find it's a cold hard world out there, and you need to do whatever you need to do, to get ahead. I don't particularly like what I'm doing, but I have a wife and two girls to support, so I'll do whatever I need to do."

I had the perfect reply. "Well, Jim, that's the difference between you and me. I'm not worried about getting ahead, because I know what I'm capable of. But I believe the smell of success would have a pretty rancid odor, if you had to look back on all of the behinds you had to kiss to get there. When I get there, it's going to smell good! Because I worked hard and earned it."

At that, Jim took off like a rocket. During the rest of the work day, if Jim ever found he was approaching me, he would turn sharply and go the other way. I think I may have hit a nerve!

As they do, the years passed quickly. I believe it was about seven years later I encountered Jim again. I was working in the appliance department of Montgomery Ward. One day, I could see Jim approaching me. "You are a hard man to find," he said as he walked up to greet me. "I've spent over a year, looking to find you. One place said, 'He used to work here, but he went somewhere else.' I've literally been all over this city trying to find you Joe." He then said, "I did you a great injustice when you worked with me at Sears. I've been trying to find you so I could ask for your forgiveness."

I said, "Jim, no apology is necessary. In fact, you did me a favor. You caused me to open my eyes and see my efforts were only spinning my wheels, as I don't drink. I had wasted a year and seven months of my life, believing I could get ahead. I should be thanking you."

"You don't know what a load of guilt it takes off of me, hearing you say that." Then he said, "I don't know if you are aware of it or not, but I quit my job at Sears." (This was quite a surprise, as I had been told he had been promoted and was making very good pay.) "I quit for the same reason you did. I got tired of kissing behinds!" Then he said, "Also, I don't know if you heard or not, but my wife divorced me. She hired a detective to follow me and get evidence of my cheating on her."

I said, "I'm so sorry to hear that, Jim."

With a big smile that lit up his face, very excitedly he said, "But fortunately through the grace of Jesus Christ, she remarried me!"

Jim then went on to tell me of his walk through darkness and his coming to the light of God's love and forgiveness.

"Joe, I'd been such a fool, letting satan guide my life. When my wife left me, I called to work sick for two weeks. My wife and kids meant the world to me, and because I'd messed up, now they were gone. I spent the first week getting drunk and feeling sorry for myself. But as the second week started, I remembered something my mother had told me.

'If you ever find yourself in trouble and you don't know what to do, consult God, read His Word, and you will find the answers you need.' I dusted off my Bible and began doing what my mother had told me to do. Joe, it was *amazing*! I would ask God a question, then open my Bible, and there in front of me was the answer I needed. It took me several months to convince my wife I was a newly born Christian man. But eventually she believed me, and we remarried. I am now studying to become a minister!"

All I could say was, "*Wow!*"

Jim got a part-time job, working at the Wards store with me. We would take turns taking one another to lunch. He even invited me to come hear him preach, which I did. He did a good job. Who would ever have predicted we would become close friends? Only God could have been behind such a thing.

One day, I learned Jim had taken a job as pastor of a church in Jacksonville. The last I heard was that Jim had died. (He had a few years on me.) But what a happy ending his life had! Death had no sting for his widow and his girls. I so hope this true story ministers to the heart of any dealing with unfaithfulness or alcohol. God is so loving, faithful, and full of mercy. How and why would anyone reject His Son, Jesus?

CHAPTER 9

One More Alcohol and Me: True Story

This story is of the kind of man I have been, regarding people trying to impose alcohol on me. Every word is true. It describes what happened during an actual event in my life. I hope you enjoy.

I was working at Wards at the time. It was time for the Annual Awards Banquet. It was to be held in Tampa at the Hawaiian Inn. Dinner was served, along with the hula dancers and fire dancers. Overall, it was quite a nice evening.

As we were going to Tampa, proceeding from the store, the department manager invited me, along with our two other salesmen to ride along with him. I was not sure about giving up my freedom to leave at my will. But the manager assured me after the awards were over, he would be directly returning to the store. I could save on gas and share in fellowship with my co-workers. So I agreed on that basis. Little did I know he had lied to me.

The awards ceremony was a very entertaining one. We won a few awards and were happy about that. But once the ceremony had ended, I found the manager and the other two guys did not want to immediately return to the store. Instead, as it was only a short distance away, it was decided to celebrate by going to the 2100 Odyssey Club, which was a strip joint. I tried to protest but was accused of being an old man. We had won some awards; now it was time to celebrate.

I felt a queasiness within my stomach the moment we drove on to the parking lot. I knew inside I did not belong there. Still, as we often do, I went along with the guys. What else could I do? I was thinking. The music was loud, and the gyrating girls made it a point to do so in front of our table. As they did, my fellow employees grinned sheepishly, as they put ten and twenty dollar bills into the girl's bra and/or panties. Sorry, not me, I'm not so hard up or easily taken in.

We did however have to order drinks, with a two drink minimum. So I ordered my usual, a coke. All was going OK, until I noticed my co-worker next to me on my right, attempting to pour some of his drink into my coke. I calmly looked over at him and said, "You don't want to do that."

"Why not?" He challenged.

"Because if you try it, I will take you outside and beat the hell out of you, and your evening would be spoiled, because you would be in a lot of pain."

"Is that a threat?" He sarcastically asked.

I said, "No, my friend, I don't believe in threats. It's a cold, hard, and very painful fact of life. If you keep on pushing for it, you will know exactly what that means to you."

At this, I told the manager I needed to speak with him privately. He stepped with me to the entrance area. There I told him the following. "Bob, I'm a Christian, and I don't feel comfortable being here in this environment. Besides, that moron is likely to try pouring something into my coke. If he does, I won't say a word to him. I will just simply beat the hell out of him. So I've decided I need to head for home."

"I understand, Joe," he said. "But how will you get there?"

"I'll call and ask my sister if she would come and give me a ride back to the store. I'm sure she will."

"OK, I'll tell the guys you were feeling sick."

I angrily said, "You can tell them anything you want. I'm out of here!"

At this, I turned and walked out the door, not looking back. As I walked up Dale Mabry, looking for a place where I might find a pay phone, I noticed an all-night bowling center. I went inside, found the phone, and made my call. It was around 2:00 a.m., and both my sister and grandmother were asking me why and what had happened to my car. I said I'd explain when I got home. Then I rented a lane and began to throw the bowling ball very hard at the pins. I was taking out the anger and aggression I felt toward me, for having been so ignorant to have trusted that manager.

All turned out good. My explanation to my family was greeted with praise to God that I had made such a wise decision. At work, it was another story. Several of the guys could not resist teasing me about not being able to hold my coke. I let them have their little laugh, knowing it came from their ignorance. But would you believe it? There was one guy who did not tease me; he chose instead to thank me.

It was the one whom I had told I would beat the hell out of. He came to me and said, "I hear I got a little out of hand yesterday evening. I'm sorry for that, and I want to thank you for leaving as you did. Joe, please don't tell anyone I said this. But I do believe you really would have beat the hell out of me, had I tried again to pour alcohol into your coke. Thank you for caring about me enough to not let that happen."

Kind of a dramatic story? Almost unbelievable? But as a little boy, I was taught to be true to my Irish and Kentuckian heritage. I was told to never ever be a bully. *But,* if some moron wanted to bully me, I must not walk away, until I found out who won the fight. This good advice kept me from having to actually fight several bullies in my life. They are basically cowards. When they learn you are willing to fight back, they get afraid of the physical damage you might do to them, and they will either run away or sincerely apologize for having bothered you. I've experienced this several times in my life. Amen.

CHAPTER 10

Update: My Fourth Death Proclamation Is Issued

I guess it's time to bring you up to date. As of the time I am writing this book, I have been told by the kidney specialist that I most likely won't live through this year 2016. As this is mid-October, that does not sound good. But, as my faith is in God and His timing, I have no fear of what man says. As a matter of fact, this is the fourth death decree I have been given by the various doctors. As long as I am able to complete the work God has assigned for me to do, I will rest easy when the end comes.

In the first week of September, I went to see my primary care doctor at the VA. I was trying to use a variety of vitamins to flush out my kidneys. But the result was constipation and stomach pains. I brought with me the vitamins I had been taking for only a short while, asking his recommendations. Dr. Z. then informed me that my kidneys were operating at only 75 percent. The vitamins were causing a sludge-like backup. This was why the problem came to be. Dr. Z. told me he would arrange a telephone consultation for me on Tuesday with the kidney specialist. He said he knows more about vitamins and could give me the information I needed. This was on Friday of the week.

Sure enough when Tuesday came, I received the awaited call. It was not what I had been expecting. The doctor stated that Dr. Z. had given me the wrong figures. He said he had looked at my blood test and found my kidneys were operating at only 13 percent. He said I was in need of immediate chemo treatment. He said it might even be too late, and at 10 percent is when they recommended a colostomy bag. He offered to place me in the hospital (add) "for a period of 14 to 15 days, to conduct tests, then begin chemo treatment. I told him of my faith in God. His reply was, "Here's what I'm willing to do. My team and I will be happy to assist you with the needed chemo. But, if you don't want it, just say so, and I won't bother or call you again."

I thought rather abrupt and to the point. Hearing my functioning go from 75 percent down to 13 percent in just a few days was quite a shock to me. So in thinking about it, I said, "I do appreciate your honesty and directness, as apparently no one else has been telling me the truth. So I believe I will take you up on your offer."

He said, "Good," and he would make the necessary arrangements for Friday.

Shortly after having hung up the phone, I began to feel remorse for what I had done. It carried deep in my heart throughout that day. The next day found me in deep repentance to God. "Father, You said You would never leave me or forsake me. True to Your Word, You haven't. Why then would I choose to leave and forsake You? Why would I desire putting my faith in chemo rather than You, who have let me live in victory thus far?"

I called the VA hospital and was able to reach the nurse involved in setting things up for Friday. I told her how I realized now was not the time in my life for me to be forsaking my Lord, God, and Father. He has brought me this far by faith. I do not wish to abandon my faith in Him for any drug. So I'll have to cancel out for tomorrow. She tried to tell me it was vitally important to my continued living, for me to do the chemo. I said, "No, it's not. What I need most in my life is my continued faith in my God and His perfect love for me. Chemo has no love for me. My body is a temple of God's Holy Spirit, and I need to be careful about allowing drugs into it, especially any that would take away from my faith in my Father."

The nurse said, "Please come in for the chemo. The doctor said without it, you will not live to see 2017."

I replied, "That's what the doctor said. Let's see what God has to say." Again she begged me to take the chemo. I told her since I had long ago given up religion, for relationship with my Father in Heaven, my body had become a temple of His Holy Spirit, and I had the privilege of approaching Him in His throne room, and making my petitions know to Him. When even after me telling her this, she persisted in encouraging me to go for the chemo. I said, "Let me tell you about my Father. He is known as God *Almighty*! He is not Almighty, because He needs chemo to perform miracles. All He needs to do is tell the problem to depart from my body, and it's gone!"

At this, she finally said, "I understand. I'll cancel the room."

I said, "Good! Give it to someone who needs it. That's not me!"

It is so much fun, using the gift of faith I was given at birth. First, I used it to find the one *true* God, rejecting all of the phony and powerless gods of satan and man's imagination. Then I discovered

He had created me to share a loving relationship, not religion, with Him. Lastly, Jesus, His only begotten Son, had suffered and died in my place, taking on all of the punishment I was due for my sins, not just to save my soul from hell but to restore my relationship to purity in the eyes of my Heavenly Father. Now, as satan was desiring to destroy my life, what a wonderful time to use that powerful gift once more, letting my Father know He had not given me faith in vain. It's so simple and so easy. All we need to do is to place our trust in His perfect love for us and be willing to submit to His will for our life. How can that be difficult, when the key ingredient our God is made of is *love*!

CHAPTER 11

Man Who Hears from God

There are two other amazing stories which happened to me way before I had my present encounters with cancer and kidney failure. I would like to share them with you now, to hopefully increase your faith, as they have mine. The first happened about twenty years ago and had a profound effect on my faith in the loving relationship I share daily with Father God.

One day as I was studying my Bible, I came across 1 John 4:18. I don't know how many times I had either read or heard this particular passage before. But this time it was special, as the Holy Spirit taught me the real meaning of the words I had read. Here is what the scripture says, "There is no fear in love; but perfect love cast out fear: because fear has torment. He that fears is not made perfect in love."

Such powerful truth is contained in that passage. The Holy Spirit spoke to my spirit, asking me just two questions. In my answers, I learned the powerful meaning for my life is found in what I had just read. The Holy Spirit first asked, "Joe, do you realize there is not one fraction of a moment in your life, when your Heavenly Father's love for you is not perfect?" Thinking about the truthfulness and power of that spiritual fact made me more in awe of the greatness of the love my Father has for me. With thankfulness, I welcomed that teaching into my heart.

Then the Holy Spirit asked, "So, what is there to ever be fearful of, have worry, stress, anxiety, or doubts about?" I realized the answer was simple.

I answered, "*Nothing!*" That answer has by faith stayed with me. It has seen me through many storms and trials in my life, even the four death sentences issued to me by my doctors. But here's "the good news." This very same truth applies to you, as you enjoy and appreciate each day, the loving relationship (not religion) which Jesus came to restore between us and our Father in heaven. The covering of the precious blood of our Savior makes us perfect and sinless in our Father's sight! Through this power, we can daily enjoy the relationship our

Heavenly Father created us to know and share with Him.

If you will just hold on to this truth with unwavering faith, you will find there is nothing so bad in your life, which if you ask in prayer, believing in your Father's perfect love, He will not see you through. This is such a powerful truth I am sharing. Please grab on to it and never let go! Do you realize how many people not knowing the beauty and power of this truth choose out of fear and torment to end their life (which they have not the authority to do)? If only they had known and received this powerful truth from God's word and planted it deep within their heart!

Trusting in our Father's perfect love with unshakable faith, satan will never be able to replace our faith with fear and torment. Oh the unimaginable *love* our Father has for each of us, His creation, whom He created to share daily in a deep and loving relationship. In creating us, God gave us something even the angels do not possess. He breathed His very own breath into our body, giving us a living soul. Our soul, made of His breath, gives us relationship with God and authority over the angels in heaven, the safe journey home for our soul, God placed in the hands of our spirit, which is our free will.

All of this is part of God having made us in His image; we have a body, soul, and spirit. Our free will (spirit) is where the problem lies. God's word states that there is a constant battle between our flesh and its desires and those desires of our spirit. We may choose to accept or reject Jesus, God's Son and our Redeemer. Or we may choose to thankfully, with a happy heart, welcome Him to take away all of our sins and give us His Holy Spirit to dwell within.

It is our need to daily yield our spirit (our will) to that of the Holy Spirit. But the desires of our flesh are strong, with a hunger for what the world has to offer. There is a verse in God's word, which many have been taught is a means of making God into our personal genie. "Honor the Lord in all of your ways, and He will give you the desires of your heart." Some believe with a con artist effort to make God think they are wanting to honor Him, He will give them whatever their heart desires. That is a lie from satan!

The reality of this powerful verse is if we willingly submit our spirit (our free will), to that of the Holy Spirit (God's Will), He will guide us as to what our heart wishes to desire. For example, we will choose to start our day by seeking to dwell within the kingdom of God, rather than that of the world. This is how we can be in the world yet not of its sinful system. As we ask for and permit the Holy Spirit (God's Will) to be our spiritual guide in all we think, do, and say, we may work toward becoming holy, as our Father in heaven is holy. The holy fruit of the Spirit of Truth will more freely flow. All that is needed is for us to choose to crucify the will of our flesh. This is to simply sacrifice our flesh to the love of God. Jesus said, "If you love me, keep my commandments." They are far easier to keep, with the Holy Spirit, rather than our flesh in charge of what we desire.

My friends, sharing this powerful teaching which I received from the Holy Spirit is part of the reason why God has kept me alive. He has been answering the sincere prayers of repentance; I, His most unfaithful of servants, have prayed and do pray daily. For decades, I refused to answer His call to get involved in His ministry. As I stated earlier, when we were approaching the year 2000, the Holy Spirit spoke to me, asking, "Joe, do you realize you are on your way to spending your eternity among the poorest of souls in heaven?" Shocked by this news, I asked why. "Because for decades, you have run away from my call to use you in My ministry."

I knew at once this was true, for I had many times heard His call to enter into ministry and be used by Him. But I would say, "Maybe later. Right now I'm too busy enjoying what the world has to offer me." Realizing the future which could be awaiting me in eternity, as I had been warned, I wanted to change that prospect. So I prayed, asking that before I must die, God would use me mightily for His honor and glory. Then realizing how much my life paralleled that of St. Paul. I changed my prayer to be: "Lord, please do for me, what You did for St. Paul. Take this chief of sinners of his day (me) and turn my life around. Before I die, use me mightily for Your honor and glory. Make of me one of Your success stories."

The blessings of hearing the Holy Spirit's voice happened in a big way, fifteen years ago. Having very bad congestion in my throat, I decided to go to the triage part of the VA to obtain immediate help in getting it out of my body. What I was unaware of was that the day before, one of their co-workers had dropped dead in front of them. The cause was untreated high blood pressure. Now I was quite a bit overweight back then, weighing in at 265 pounds.

When I got to see the doctor assigned to treat me, he said, "Your blood pressure is up a little too high for me to be comfortable with. So, what I'm going to do is order an EKG for you, to make sure your heart is OK. Then based on information the EKG reveals, I will do one of two things. I will either give you medication and send you home or keep you in the hospital overnight for observation."

After the EKG had been done, I waited to hear from the doctor the results. Upon receiving the results, I was both shocked and surprised by the news. "Mr. Callihan, it looks as if you either are or recently have had a heart attack."

I objected to this idea. "I've not had any pain or numbness. Besides, I'm only fifty-seven years old. I'm too young to be having a heart attack."

"Nevertheless," the doctor said, "we prefer to err on the side of caution. So I'm going to put a heart monitor on you and keep you overnight, just to make sure you are alright."

I agreed and thanked the doctor for caring.

I got set up in my room, which I shared with three others, at around seven p.m. Soon, a heart specialist arrived to inform me of his opinion. He, like the MD, said I either was having or recently had a heart attack. He had gained his perspective through studying my EKG information, as well as the high blood pressure reading. He said he was going to prescribe I'd be given a shot of medication which would slow down my heart rate and prevent me having any more of a heart attack. But what if I'm not having a heart attack? I asked would this do more harm than good? I was not at all comfortable with the answer he gave me. "There is a possible risk to every medication." As the nurse went to prepare the shot, I prayed, asking that it do no harm to this temple of the Holy Spirit.

It became time to go to sleep. My grandmother had me read the ninety-first Psalm to her every night. As the result, I had it memorized. So I began to recite its powerful truths in behalf of myself. The closing verse states: "With long life will I satisfy him and show him My salvation." I said to Father God, "Lord, I don't mean to be complaining. But today, fifty-seven is not considered to be a long life, perhaps one hundred and seven, but fifty-seven is still young."

At this, the Holy Spirit spoke to me and said the following: "Joe, there is nothing wrong with your heart. They are mistaken. You shall live a long and fruitful life. So have no fear. I am with you. Your body is My temple. Angels are guarding and protecting you."

At around a little after midnight, I felt sick. I went into the bathroom and coughed up two large fur balls of phlegm. Seeing them, I began to praise and thank God. The nurse who happened to have come in to check on us handed me a wet washcloth. Then puzzled at my reaction, she asked, "You're thanking God for that?"

I said, "Yes, what you see there is the reason why I am in here. I can breathe easy now."

The time passed, and at around two a.m., they came to take me for a sonogram of my heart. Then at four o'clock, I was awakened and told it was time for my next shot to slow down my heart rate. I reacted to this news by saying, "Sorry, but I don't want or need your shot."

"Oh no!" they proclaimed. "You must allow us to give you this shot. Otherwise you may die of a heart attack, and we would not want to see that happen."

"You don't need to worry, that's not going to happen," I replied.

"Please Mr. Callihan, let us give you the shot, and you can go back to sleep."

"Look," I said, "I've heard from God, and He said you are mistaken. There is nothing wrong with my heart. It is perfectly fine. So I don't want or need your shot."

From me having stated that I had heard from God, their reaction was, "This guy's delusional. Or worse, he's insane." They threatened by saying, "We'll have to tell the doctor, if you don't let us give you this shot."

I said, "That's a good idea! Tell the doctor. Tell your mother and father. You can even tell your grandparents if you like. But I'm telling you, as the patient, I have the right to refuse to allow you to give me that shot. Give it to yourself, if you must! But you are *not* giving it to me! Understand?"

Finally, at around ten a.m., the doctor showed up, as she was making her rounds. Two of the nurses excitedly ran up to her and exclaimed, "Doctor, Mr. Callihan would not allow us to give him the shot to slow down his heart rate! Then making the pointed finger circling gesture at the side of their head, they said, "He thinks he heard from God. And God said his heart is fine. We made a mistake!"

The doctor turned toward them and said, "He's right!" Walking over to my bed, she told me, "Mr. Callihan, this morning, I got to examine both your sonogram and your EKG. I discovered your heart is indeed in good health. What you had is called a false positive. Sometimes when you are a bit overweight, when laying on your side, it will pinch a nerve and create a blip on the EKG which looks like a heart attack. So you did well in refusing to take that shot."

The look on the faces of those nurses was priceless. I feel so sorry for those only having powerless religion and those who do not know or cannot bring themselves to calling God, Father. To them, He is known only as "the Man upstairs." How empty and how it shows lack of relationship, just simple-minded religion, as their guide.

This true story I have just shared is not to glorify me as something special. What happened in hearing the voice of the Holy Spirit is what God desires for all of His children to experience on a daily basis. It is when religion denies the Holy Spirit the opportunity to teach and bring gifts of power to the redeemed children of God; such a weakness of not believing you could actually hear God's voice is part of their life. If this kind of lack applies to you? You need to ask yourself what are you going to do to gain the power God desires for you to possess, as you share in your loving relationship and not religion with Him? Amen!

CHAPTER 12

Hurt Feelings, Misconceived Pride, and Unusual Man of God

I have shared with you from the medical perspective. Now I must tell you of the spiritual side of this amazing experience. It is so important to clearly hear, listen, and follow, as the Holy Spirit leads us. Here is where I encountered hurt feelings and misconceived beliefs, regarding my seemingly "prideful" attitude. All of it reflects the price I was called upon to pay, in order to uphold my faith in God alone, as my source for healing.

When at the VA, I first turned down the chemo, expressing my faith in God's perfect love for me; I heard the Holy Spirit tell me how I was to behave now and in the future. I was to let no one but Father God receive *all* of the credit for how I receive my healings. I understood at once; it was and is a personal thing between my faith in His perfect love for me and His plans to use me as His servant. This occasionally caused me some degree of misunderstanding among a few pastors who wanted to pray for my healing.

Several times, when being called up for prayer, I specifically would ask the pastor not to pray for my healing of cancer (never mentioning the diabetes I was told I also had), as God was already doing what needed to be done. Most understood, even though some had their feeling hurt, at my request. But there was one pastor I encountered one Sunday, who apparently felt led to ignore the request I had made before the service started.

Not having attended his church for some time, before the service, I approached him. I simply asked if I might bring the congregation up to date as to what had been happening. I then said, "I do not require your laying of your hands on me to pray for my healing. This is to be between me using my gift of faith and what God alone can and will do. No man is to receive credit." He said he agreed, and I believed him.

However, after giving my updated testimony, this pastor had gotten behind me. Placing his hands on my shoulders, he called for the members in his church to come forward to lay hands on me and pray for Joe's healing. I was immediately upset by this betrayal. The gathering people, unaware of my earlier request, began to reach out to glum on to me and pray (however well intended) for my healing. I knew at once I was now under great pressure. I also was very disappointed at this obvious ambush by the pastor. I knew I had a decision to make. Was I to stand still and allow him to merchandise me for show? Or must I insist that God alone receive all the praise, honor, and glory for my healing?

As I had steadfastly refused allowing doctors to administer chemo, I believed I must likewise not allow any pastor to be able to use me to claim, "Of course Joe got healed. 'I' laid 'my' hands on him, and 'I' prayed for him to be healed. God answered 'my' prayer!"

A bold thought entered my mind. "Not with me you don't!" So as he, having his hands on my shoulders, opened his mouth to begin to pray and curse the cancer, and me being obedient to the Holy Spirit, I abruptly shouted out saying, "*No!*" I then walked calmly away from him and the people. Stepping down from the altar and taking a seat in a nearby pew, I waited for the service to start. I could see the look of shock on the faces of the congregation, as if in disbelief of what they had just witnessed.

I was really upset by this pastor's choice of words and action. I believe he thought I would be under stress to give in and would, allowing him to pray for my healing, making merchandise of me before all assembled there. But I chose obeying the Holy Spirit, as I will every time! I feel certain everyone in that place thought I was suffering from an overdose of pride, perhaps even thinking to their self, "With such a 'prideful attitude,' surely cancer will overtake this poor man."

I said nothing and did not want to get into any discussion, regarding what had taken place. So as soon as the service was over, I left and have never returned again to that church or pastor.

I truly desire for every reader to understand the truth of my testimony. All of my various healings have come from God Almighty *alone*, not from me nor any man! To God *alone* belongs the glory, honor, and praise for my healings.

CHAPTER 13

Chemo: The "Miracle" Drug

On occasion, I have encountered fans of chemotherapy as a way of defeating cancer. These are usually well-meaning Christians, who either personally, or know of someone that has been cured of cancer using chemotherapy. They will bluntly challenge my having asked, "What's wrong with placing your gift of faith, solely in your Creator? Is He not the Lord, God, who created everything, both the seen and the unseen? Is He not our loving Father, who made us in His image, to share each day of our life, in a loving relationship with Him (rather than an empty-headed and powerless man made 'religion')? Did He not create our physical body, which houses our soul and spirit, to become the temple of His Holy Spirit, upon our becoming born again? Lastly, is it a lie that by the stripes from the cat o' nine tails, inflicted on Jesus's body, our body can find the healing we need?"

OK, so what's wrong· with trusting· in chemo? As noted, there are some Christians who do get healed. As far as I can tell, one thing is out of place in that scenario. All of the truths from God's word, as stated above, often get denied or worse, yet, swept under the carpet. Those who are healed will be quick to proclaim how "chemo," the *"miracle"* drug, brought healing of cancer to their body. In other words, a simple-minded drug, invented by man, usurps the honor and glory belonging only to God.

But why did it work? Has anyone ever considered that Father God's perfect love is only one aspect of His being? Have we not learned of His mercy (which endures forever) and His grace (which is unmerited favor)? These also are a part of our loving Father's makeup. In many cases, He looks and sees in the life of His follower, faith like that of the apostles who were driven by fear. Remember the apostles that were with Him in the boat on the Sea of Galilee, when a tremendous storm arose? How fearful they were of perishing, even though Jesus was in the boat with them. They chose to awaken Jesus from His sleep. What was His response to them? "Oh you of little faith."

But did Jesus get angry with them? Did He allow them to continue suffering in fear? No! As we know, Jesus stood up and spoke to the storm, and it immediately ceased to be. Jesus did so, not as the result of the faith the apostles had demonstrated. As we already know, He chastised them for their lack of faith. However, He spoke to the storm in authority, and it became calm once again. This is an example of the mercy and grace which Jesus extended to the apostles, in spite of the unbelief they had shown. Although disappointed in the lack of faith demonstrated by the apostles (they had personally witnessed Him perform countless miracles), the fact that He was the Son of God had not as yet been revealed to them by the Holy Spirit. Remember when Jesus asked of them, "Who do you say that I am?" (only Peter knew through revelation by the Holy Spirit)

When asking the Holy Spirit how to respond to this challenge, regarding some choosing chemo over faith in God alone or even along with faith, receiving healing in their body, this is the answer I received. Clearly, it is due to the mercy and grace of God, working with His perfect love, which made it possible for this miracle healing to take place. Yet we, in our flesh, are quick to not even consider God, as we placed more faith in man's chemical, than in

God's perfect love. How quickly we are willing to praise the "miracle" drug for our healing.

It has been interesting, the many responses I have received when giving my testimony about three different times having turned down chemotherapy (Twice for two different forms of cancer, and once for treatment of reported kidney failure). Among the most often heard has been, what "courage" you possess. Courage? An interesting choice of words.

The reason why this topic came into my mind was, early one morning as I was watching on Roku, one of my favorite Bible teachers, Dr. Charles Stanley. Dr. Stanley was speaking on the subject of courage. In doing so, he gave several definitions for its meaning. One was, courage is fear that has said its prayers (sounds spiritual). Another, attributed to General Patton was, courage is fear that holds on just a minute longer (sounds logical).

I got to thinking about both of these definitions, and found I was in disagreement with both. Although both sound good to our flesh. To me, both have a major flaw. What could that flaw be? Both give praise to fear, Fear, is a gift from satan and is the opposite of faith. Both cannot occupy the place of priority in our mind. It's the same as "no one can serve two masters."

Yet we so often will use words relating to what our flesh naturally perceives as a fitting description for the driving force behind some action we call courageous. I have found that in my spirit, the force behind my actions of turning down chemo, is related to my faith in my Father's Perfect love for me, and His plan for my life. The spirit perceives things of the Spirit.

My faith in God's Perfect Love has been a growing process. I did not arrive there overnight. It has been a matter of my personally knowing my Father better; through all of the years when He has, via His Spirit, guided me, and on many occasions allowed my guardian angel to save me from serious injury, or even death.

It is like Abram responded when God asked him to offer as sacrifice, the life of his only son. Abram knew God's nature was love. He knew this because of the many years he had been seeking from God, to discover a way of restoring our lost relationship with Him. I believe Abram knew in his heart, even before the Scripture was ever given, that God works all things for good to those who love Him, and are called according to His purpose.

I believe because Abram had great faith in the nature of God being love. He willingly attempted to plunge the dagger into Isaac's heart. We know

Abram's beliefs turned out to be based in fact. Because of the faith he demonstrated, God changed his name to Abraham. Which means father of faith.

I submit the ability to present what is called courage, comes not from fear, but from God's gift of faith at work in the life of the believer. If you desire more courage? May I suggest contemplating on how great is God's heart of Perfect Love for you and me. Then spend some time clearly reflecting on the many times when God, by His love, has ministered into your life. You might begin with Jesus suffering and dying in our place. When you do this, it becomes so easy to trust in that Perfect Love to see you through any storm of life, and remove any mountain.

Do I believe it is evil for a Christian to place their faith in chemotherapy? That would require judgment on my part. Authority to do that belongs to God alone, not me. I will say it is my belief that when such healing does take place in the body of one trusting in chemo, they should be mindful of the mercy and grace, along with love, which Father God extended toward them, in making this possible. Although their faith (perhaps·due to the "man-made," religious garbage teaching they have received) is not as yet to where Father God desires to see them attain, His mercy and grace, combined with His perfect love, touched their body and effected the cure they were in need of.

In closing, I would ask a serious question. What foundation can you offer as a basis to believe the power of chemo, to be a better choice than the Power of your heavenly Father's Perfect Love for you? Choosing God over chemo, does not require fear. Just the opposite, it requires using the gift of faith we are given by God at birth; and by that Faith, trusting in God's plan for your life to continue or to end. Faith or no faith, like it or not, in reality our life is in God's hands and plan, from its beginning to end.

Continue to challenge me if you wish, one who has been healed by the use of faith in God's perfect love for me alone. But now that you have read this powerful chapter, we both know the truth, as shared by the Spirit of Truth. Use chemo if you must. But be quick to give Father God all of the credits (praise, honor, and glory), for any and all healing which may take place. But also, do not blame Him, if no healing happens, and death occurs. With that advice, I shall now bring this chapter to a close. May Father God, by His Holy Spirit, through the *study* of His word, bring to each of us ever-increasing faith in Him alone. In Jesus's name, I pray.

CHAPTER 14

Faith: The Two-Sided Coin

From the beginning, I have realized my faith is a two-sided coin. One side has healing, the other death. You see, although in my prayers, my goal was to see complete healing take place in my body. I realized God's will belongs to Him alone. If this was my time to go and the means which He chose using to take me home, so it would be.

    I know my soul and spirit will not be occupying this body forever. The older I get, the closer I am to facing eternity, as we all must one day do. There will come a time of accounting before God, for the life we used our free will (guidance of our spirit) to choose living. Will we have wisely chosen Jesus and His sacrifice of love for us? Or will we in stupid pride have chosen to reject Him? Show me your faith without works; and I will by my works show you my faith. For faith without works is dead. In healing, our works consist of trusting in God's perfect will to be done regarding the outcome. Should it be His calling us home, we must not resist but welcome and honor His perfect love and will for our life.

Asking in prayers of faith, I sought healing. It is my reasons for having done so, which I believed moved God's heart. That, combined with His great mercy, grace, and perfect love, has made it possible for me to be alive and share with you this extraordinary true story. All honor and glory belong to God. I have done nothing more than use the mighty gift I was given at birth.

Here is my part of the story. I have been one of the greatest of failures to God in so many ways, each of which I have repented for. From the time of my early youth, I could hear God calling me into His ministry. But first in fear, I refused to answer, believing I was both unworthy and unequipped. My "religious teachers" failed to teach me, whom God calls He equips. So, believing in worry, fear, and doubt as to "my" ability and lack of understanding and spiritual power, I ran from God's constant call.

Then in 1974, Father God responded to me seeking understanding and spiritual power. I became born again by the Spirit of God. Speaking to me, He would remind me, "I have given you the spiritual power you claimed you lacked. When are you going to start harvesting your brothers and sisters into My kingdom?" Then to counter my fears and doubts, He would remind me that the Lord chooses to use the foolish things of the world to confound the wise. I would laugh, as I thought to myself, "It's difficult to argue with that, Lord. I don't think You could find anyone more foolish than me."

Yet sadly, hearing God's call, I would respond by saying, "I can see you using people like Gerald Derstine (my spiritual mentor), Billy Graham, Jim Bakker. They have done so much for You. Compared to them, I've done nothing." God would let me get away with using that excuse for some time. Then one day, I guess He believed it was time for me to face reality. He tripped me up with His reply, "Joe, when are you going to stop telling Me about all you have not done for Me and allow Me to use you for My honor and glory?" Also asking, "Why compare yourself to any other of My servants? It is you I have called and shall equip for ministry."

Although shook up by this statement of reality, still I ran away from answering God's call. Then one night I decided to attend a service a minister friend had encouraged me to attend. A traveling prophet had been doing the service at a local church. He was due to be there for a week, and this was his last night. I have a great deal of caution regarding those claiming to be a prophet, especially as the Bible tells us there will be many false prophets going around in the last days.

How surprised I was, when he stood before me, hand outstretched, seeking for me to arise. I did, thinking to myself, "This better be good, buddy."

He began by saying, "I was wondering when you would be attending one of these services. The Lord has a work He wants to use you to do, and you have been ignoring and putting it off. He has a message given me to share with you, and it's this. The Lord chooses to use the foolish things of the world to confound the wise. Get busy!"

I felt as if God had painted a bull's eye on my face, and this guy was an expert marksman. Well I tried but seemed to be just spinning my wheels. So once more, filled with despair, satan had me believing I was only self-called and delusional. So once more, I quit trying.

It is amazing! It now has been four years since God removed the cancerous tumors found on my liver. God could have used the other side of the coin, and I would now be four years in my grave. But in one of the Psalms I used in my prayers, it tells of how God delivered him (David) from going down into the "pit" (or as we call it, the grave). It asks,

"How could I bring you honor and praise, when deep within the grave? I am not yet in my grave. I live to bring honor and glory to my Lord, God, Holy Spirit, and Savior.

For several years, this is and has become my daily prayer. "Father, please do for me what You did for St. Paul. Take the life of this chief of sinners of his day and turn it around. Before I must die, use me, give me many legitimate reasons to permit You to say to me on the day of Judgment, 'Well done, My good and faithful servant. Enter into your reward.' Help me to be like David, oh to be considered by You to be the apple of Your eye, a man after Your heart.

Holy Spirit, please help me to be holy, as my Father in heaven is holy. Please teach, guide, and use me mightily for Your honor and glory. Father, this day I seek to dwell within Your kingdom.

Happily, I choose to deny myself. Let not my will (the desires of my spirit) be done but Your holy and perfect will (guidance of the Holy Spirit) be done in my life this day. Gladly, I choose to crucify the will and lust of my flesh. Don't allow my flesh to interfere with anything the Holy Spirit would have me think, do, or say. Father, all of this I ask, in Jesus's name, Amen."

I pray all who have read my testimony will be blessed. May you become aware of how deep and perfect your Father's love is for you. May you remove faith in the "religious man upstairs" and begin to daily enjoy via the Holy Spirit the loving relationship your Heavenly Father desires to share with you.

In closing, my recent blood test from my outside doctor revealed all is well. Every vital sign is perfect. Oh, and the kidney failure which was 13 percent in September of last year is at 17 percent. I look forward to the day when I hear 100 percent healthy. (During recent hospital stay, kidneys function was reported to be at 25 percent)

Meanwhile, may I encourage you to Google my name? You will find many of the other books I have authored, both spiritual and secular. Several more are still to come.

If you feel this book deserves it, please help me spread the word on its availability. Better yet, get a copy to share with relatives, friends, or even strangers who look like they could use encouragement to use their gift of faith. I say this not to make me rich but for both of us to have the opportunity to store up treasure in heaven.

ONE LAST REQUEST

It is my prayer this true story of what God has done in my life and in my body is an inspiration to all who read it. I have done nothing more than wisely having chosen to use the mighty gift of faith in the one true God, which I was given a measure of at birth. I have trusted completely in my Heavenly Father's will and His perfect love for me. I believed, and do believe, He had and has work for me to do, which satan has been trying to deny coming to fulfillment.

Sadly, when it comes to faith, many fail to use, while others blindly choose to misuse this gift, placing belief in nothing or one of satan's or man's false little powerless gods. Those who permit satan to feed their ego believe there could not possibly be a god greater than them. God's word proclaims anyone looking closely at the stars, planets, and universes in the night sky and declaring there is no God is foolish.

You have the many differing man- and satan-made "religions," each intended to lead us astray from knowing, believing in, loving, and serving the one true God. You have the Hindu, which believes in several thousand little false and powerless gods of man's imagination. Then there is faith in Islam. They sadly believe in a god who teaches hatred, despair, envy, and the ways of darkness and death to his followers. Christians know him by his true name—lucifer.

Equally as bad are those in bondage to the many "Christian religions." They, whose foundation is made of man-made interpretations of scripture and belief in doctrines, dogmas, and traditions of pride and division, are presenting a false body and bride of Christ to the world. They, in their errant pride in teachings which come from man, not the Holy Spirit (the Spirit of Truth, Whom they greatly fear), are the cause for those in the world looking upon Christians as just another of the world's confused "religions." We are *not* a religion and never were! We are the redeemed children of our Father in heaven.

We are redeemed by the Sacrifice of Love, made for us by Jesus, God's Son, that our *relationship* with Father God may be restored to purity in His sight. Because of Jesus, we are given His Holy Spirit, Who brings with Him the kingdom of God, when we choose to surrender all to Jesus and follow Him alone, as we permit His Holy Spirit (not man's religious beliefs) to lead and guide us into all truth.

How thankful I am that at the age of thirty, I was delivered from the "religion" I grew up in. Now, living daily in my relationship with my Father, Whose love for me is perfect, I am free to enjoy the life I was created to know and share with my Father each day of my life. His Holy Spirit has even taught me how to choose dwelling in the Secret Place of the Most High, abiding under God's shadow and being covered by His wings each new day. The Secret Place of the Most High is His kingdom within. It is within all who have been born again by God's Holy Spirit and walk not after the flesh but after the Spirit (having crucified the lust of the flesh). It is within us; we need to learn how to dwell within it. (Please check out *Fill Me with the Fire of Your Love*, by Carlote Bengemyere, to learn how this is possible.)

I would ask that in love, you help spread the word regarding these miracles of healing, wrought by the power of faith in the perfect love of the one true God for His own, that acknowledge Him. Please tell your friends, loved ones, neighbors, and even strangers, who might be in need of knowledge of how deep and perfect is their Father's love for them. Let them know of my true testimony. All not to lift me up but for the honor and glory of the one true God. It is by, through, and in His perfect love that I live, breathe, move, and have my being. The same applies to all who place their faith in Jesus and His Sacrifice of Love made in their behalf.

In closing, I would like to share with you three powerful Psalms which I received from the Holy Spirit. May you enjoy and be blessed.

The Only Thing Left to Do

The only thing left to do
In a feeble voice they say
Is call upon God's mercy
I guess it's time to pray

The only thing left is prayer
All other sources exhausted
"Maybe" God will hear your cry
He even "might" be trusted

To experience the power of prayer
Only *faith* can pay the cost
But when the only thing left is prayer
Faith is all but lost

"Why is it that you ask me
Doubting what I may do?
How little religion has taught about
My Agapé love for you"

Prayer is an only thing
When faith is absent from it
Prayer sent toward heaven without faith
To earth will quickly plummet

JOSEPH CALLIHAN

Growing Faith

Faith is a great blessing
A seed God places in each heart
Helping lead us to our Savior
His mercy, grace, and love to impart

Although Faith at first is tiny
Like a mustard seed you know
As we seek to know our Father
As a tree our Faith will grow

Growing is a process
Taking years of tears and pain
Learning who we are in Christ
Growing Faith we shall attain

Putting on the mind of Christ
Takes Faith which is mature
Loving others just like Jesus
Gives us power to be pure

The world does not love our Savior
Neither does it love us too
As we seek the Holy Spirit's guidance
He will teach us what to say and do

For we just like our Savior
Can overcome the world
By His blood and our testimony
God's kingdom is unfurled

When we choose to use and take Faith with us
From cradle to the grave
We show our Father we are thankful
For this mighty gift He gave

JOSEPH CALLIHAN

I CRY OUT

I CRY OUT IN THE EARTH
THAT TREMBLES
I CRY OUT IN THE WINDS THAT BLOW
I CRY OUT IN THE RAGING WATERS
IN VOLCANOS, FIRE, AND SNOW

I CRY IN THE NAME OF JUSTICE
I CRY FOR THE INNOCENT DEAD
WHY DO YOU LOVE AND
SERVE THE DARKNESS?
MUST JUDGMENT FALL
UPON YOUR HEAD?

I CRY OUT IN THE NAME OF BABIES
MURDERED IN THEIR MOTHER'S WOMB
HOW YOUR HEARTS HAVE HARDENED
LETTING satan LEAD YOUR
SOUL TO DOOM

WHAT WILL IT TAKE FOR
YOU TO HEAR ME
AND RESPOND UNTO MY CALL
TO A NATION THAT ONCE LOVED ME
I SAY: RETURN TO ME OR FALL!

I SPEAK NOW UNTO MY SERVANTS
WHO DAILY CALL TO ME
ARISE IN LOVE MY MIGHTY ARMY
GO AND SET THE CAPTIVES FREE!

HOW MUCH LONGER MUST I CRY OUT?
HOW MUCH LOUDER MUST I SHOUT?
WILL YOU SURRENDER ALL TO satan
OR BY MY SPIRIT CAST HIM OUT?

TO THOSE WHO TRULY LOVE ME
AND WALK IN LIBERTY
USE THE POWER THAT IS IN YOU
TURN THIS COUNTRY BACK TO ME

UNDER GOD YOU ONCE DID
PLEDGE THIS NATION
PRAYER TO ME WAS IN YOUR SCHOOL
IN GOD WE TRUST WAS
BOLDLY ON YOUR MONEY
AND YOU TAUGHT THE GOLDEN RULE

OH HOW FAR YOU HAVE
STRAYED FROM ME
FROM THE TRUTH, THE LIFE, THE WAY
HOW MUCH LONGER MUST I CRY OUT?
REPENT! RETURN TO ME THIS DAY

JOSEPH CALLIHAN

FOR I YOUR GOD AM JEALOUS
OF THE GODS YOU HAVE
PLACED IN FRONT OF ME
IF YOU CONTINUE TO CHOOSE
AND SERVE THEM
YOU NO LONGER SHALL BE FREE

HOW LOUDLY MUST I CRY OUT?
HOW LONG WILL I LET
MOCKERY GO ON?
WHEN WILL YOU SEEK MY MERCY
AND REPENT FROM DOING WRONG?

THE TIME IS GROWING SHORTER
TO RESPOND UNTO MY VOICE
WHO IS YOUR LORD AND MASTER?
SOON YOU MUST MAKE YOUR CHOICE

MY PERSONAL CONFESSION

It is with deep trepidation and concern that I dare to reveal the following. In fact, I had somewhat of a mild debate with the Holy Spirit, regarding my doing so. I felt led that He would have me share, in spite of the fact that many possessing only powerless man-made "religion" and not restored relationship may tend to not understand things of a deep spiritual nature. Many might think the man who wrote this testimony of true events in his life is one living in an episode of *The Twilight Zone*.

Yet due to the Holy Spirit (as always) having won the debate, here it goes. I pray all reading this will understand fully its meaning. I must go back into an incident which happened in my past. It is something I feel both sorrow and joy over. I know that sounds impossible. But please wait until you have finished reading what I am about to share.

It was just over three decades ago satan sent into my life for a brief period a demon-possessed woman. Sadly, at the time, I lacked discernment to know this was so. However, as it turned out, she was sent not to destroy me and the ministry God was birthing in me but rather that of an already powerful man of God.

This young lady was physically very attractive, from head to toes. I can't remember exactly how it was that I began to date her. But we did briefly date, only as friends. She appeared to be almost angelic in her facial and overall beauty. Adding to that, she was a composer of her own praise songs (a psalmist). She could play guitar and sing with a clarity resembling that of crystal bells ringing. The words of praises to God seemed so beautiful.

However, as I said, she managed to destroy the ministry of another. About six months into our dating, I introduced her to my pastor friend. They immediately hit it off, as she was so charming and disarming. In fact, I was there when she offered to voluntarily help my pastor friend, by doing secretarial work for him. His wife had been doing the work for years. But it was agreed it would be nice to take some of the load off of her, so she may have more time to enjoy her life.

It started out as innocent but did not take long, before the pastor was supposedly caught in a compromising position with this girl. Although he fought to deny the charges brought against him, in the end he lost his credentials as a minister and sadly also lost his wife of over thirty years, as she divorced him. The girl kind of disappeared, and I never have seen her since.

Why would I go to the trouble of relating all of this to you? It is simply because of something unique, which this demon-possessed woman did for me. But first, I guess I'd better explain further how it was that I discovered she was actually working for satan. Sometime after the incident with the pastor, I was playing a cassette tape she had given me of some of her songs. She had told me she recorded on the one side only. So always I would play what was on that side and then rewind.

However, one day after the pastor incident happened, it occurred to me to try playing the other side of the tape, just to see if perhaps she had recorded more songs. What a *shock*! Ever heard the term "backward masking"? On that opposite side were her saying praises to satan. The music was coming out garbled.

But her voice and words were clear and easy to understand. What was it she was saying? "satan,

satan, I love you. satan, I live to serve you. satan, you alone are my master." This was repeatedly heard in the background. Though the musical sounds were jumbled, her words of praise to satan, and pride in serving him, could be heard very clearly.

Friends, backward masking is *real!* I still have that tape somewhere, although I never have the desire to "play it again, satan." How I do wish I had played it, before introducing her to my pastor. The gift of spiritual discernment is so important for us to desire to receive from Father God, especially these days!

Now it is time to hold on to your hat! Would you believe? This demon-possessed woman actually gave me a spiritually correct interpretation of a dream I had, which I shared with her? One day, while on a date, I related to her a recent dream I had encountered during the night, although I did not know it then. Today, her interpretation has come true, much to my amazement.

MY DREAM

I spoke of how in my dream, I had seen many people in a park setting, flying effortlessly through the air. Not for great distances, but in leaps and bounds of a hundred yards or less. They (like the fictional character Superman), would take a bounding step forward as their body left the ground, and they would sometimes go as high as a hundred feet above the ground. Traveling only a short distance, before gently gliding back down, to repeat the steps again and again. I joyfully watched as parents would take their little ones by the hand, and teach how to fly along with them. Somehow I knew what I was witnessing was due to my having taught them to fly just as I could do.

THE INTERPRETATION SHE GAVE

After sharing this dream, this demon possessed woman gave me the following interpretation. You are being used by God to teach people how to escape the bondage of depression, anxiety, worry, doubt, and fear, which hold down the freedom of their spiritual growth. They are flying, because they have chosen to let the Holy Spirit teach and lead them, as He guides their life. He alone, is giving them the desires of their heart, and no other source may interfere. As I had noticed the smiles of joy on each face. She said it was the joy imparted by acknowledging the kingdom of God reigning within.

I must admit I liked what I heard, and was impressed by it. But, over the passing of many years, until now, I have yet to see it come to pass. If you can grasp the foundational spiritual power contained in my testimony. Then you, like me, will be set free from the bondage of fear, anxiety, worry, depression, and all other demons. Their goal is to attack your faith in God's love, and cause the loss of your inheritance of the kind of joy which passes human understanding, regardless what mountains (obstacles) satan may be confronting us with. We can easily remove, or fly over every one, by holding on with faith to a powerful truth.

Would you like to learn how to fly? Know the POWER of this truth: Father God's Love for us is **Perfect**, EVERY MOMENT OF OUR LIFE! This being a truth we can stand on, may I dare to ask: What is there for us to fear, or have worry, doubts, depression, or anxiety about? NOTHING! Once you believe this to be a true and deep spiritual reality for the redeemed of the Lord. You will find your ability to gain spiritual maturity will begin to soar!

I pray all reading this confession will be blessed by grasping the truth it teaches. Please do not allow man's "religious beliefs" and powerless teachings keep you from all the Holy Spirit desires to impart into your life. Then, perhaps one day I might enjoy reading your book of testimony regarding what God in His love, mercy, grace, and power, has done in your life. Till then, blessings to all!

Joe Callihan

JOSEPH CALLIHAN

HELP IS ON THE WAY

Help is on the way
I cry to You my Lord
Because I know You Love me
My plea won't be ignored

Help is on the way
The Comforter within me speaks
Wait patiently for My timing
Though is be hours, days, or weeks

Your deliverance draws near
Your Faith helps make it so
So put away all fear
You're My child, this you know

Have I not said: Because he has
set his love upon Me,
Therefore will I deliver him:
I will set him on high,
Because he has known My name

He shall call upon Me,
And I will answer him
I will be with him in trouble,
I will deliver him and honor him

**With long life will I satisfy him,
And show him My salvation"**

What peace and joy is mine
When to Father God I kneel and pray
Whether for my own needs or another's
I know, **Help is on the way!**

Psalm of a Man Told by Doctors He is Dying

When told you are dying
Yet you want so much to live
Just take this heavy burden
And to Jesus gladly give

Give Him all your faith
Give Him all your joy
Remember, to Father God
You are His girl or boy

Never surrender to fear satan
Nor his predictions of your doom
Remember to Jesus Christ
You are His Bride, He is your Groom

Stay in perfect peace,
For your life is in God's Plan
Be it healing or be it death
Always, you are in your Father's hand

Boldly go before your Father's throne
He is the great I Am
You shall not be called home
If it's not yet within His plan

The words to this Psalm
Which I share with you today
Come in answer to the prayers
Of one who asks: "Lord, please let me stay."

Lord, I have so much to do
To bring honor unto You
Let me live to bring You glory
In everything I say and do

May I lead all souls to Jesus
As I go along each day
Lord please hear my cry and plea
As to You I humbly pray

So many blessings many miracles
You have given in my life
I am free from cares and burdens
In this world of grief and strife

May I ask for one more miracle
satan seeks my life to take
In Your Love, Your Grace, Your Mercy
Show the world that You are Great

May I live to defeat satan
And to set the captives free
In Your Mercy, Grace, and Love
May I Your faithful servant be

Lord, attend unto my voice
I know You hear my cry and plea
Please use me in a mighty way
Before it's time to come home to Thee

How I thank You that know You
As Father, Comforter, Savior, and my Lord
Above You there is no other
To be worshipped and adored

In You alone my Lord do I breathe,
Move, and have my very being
Please give me just a little more time
Before Your presence I'll be seeing

ABOUT THE AUTHOR

Author Joe Callihan has admittedly been one of the worst failures to God. Having heard God's call to be used by Him, since a small boy, Joe ran from answering that call. Even after having become born again at age thirty and hearing the call even more strongly, Joe refused to answer, having been caught up with success in the world.

Then, as we approached the year 2000, Joe was shocked one day, when clearly and strongly he heard the Holy Spirit ask a question, "Joe, are you aware you are in danger of spending your eternity among the poorest of souls in heaven?" Shocked, Joe asked why. "For decades, you have run away from My call to use you for my honor and glory." Joe knew he was guilty as charged.

He repented, and every day he prays, asking, "Please Lord, before I must die, do for me what you did for St.

Paul. Turn my life around and use me mightily for Your honor and glory. Please make of me one of Your success stories."

Is God answering Joe's prayer? You need to only look at all of the miraculous healing which has occurred in Joe's body over the past four years. satan wants to see Joe dead that he might not accomplish what God desires. But satan is only a little snake to be stepped on.

All praise, honor, and glory belong to God the Father; Jesus, His son; and His Holy Spirit (His will)!